WOODCRAFT GIFT PROJECTS

by

RONALD P. OUIMET

JONATHAN DAVID PUBLISHERS, INC
MIDDLE VILLAGE, NY 11379

Library of Congress Cataloging in Publication Data

Ouimet, Ronald P.
    Woodcraft gift projects

    1.   Woodwork.   I.   Title.
TT180.093   684′ .08   79-15909
ISBN   0-8246-0243-9

Printed in the United States of America

CONTENTS

WOODCRAFT GIFT PROJECTS

TO CHARLOTTE

My Inspiration
And the Mother of
Our Two Daughters

ACKNOWLEDGMENTS

Grateful acknowledgment is given to Ron Fortier, Leonard Bernard, and James Whitney, associates of the National Teacher Corp Project, for their helpful suggestions and assistance in completing this manuscript. I also acknowledge David Mendelsohn for his outstanding photography.

INTRODUCTION

The projects presented in this book are geared for the advanced craftsman, but the beginning woodworker will be able to execute many without difficulty. Each woodcraft project is presented with a detailed working drawing, step-by-step instructions, and photographs.

The following basic information will prove helpful to most craftsmen.

WOODWORKING JOINTS

Most joints are held together by fasteners such as nails, screws, corrugated fasteners, wedges, or pins. Glue is used as an adhesive when a metal or wood fastener is not desired. The strength of a woodworking joint will depend largely on the accuracy of the fit and the quality of the workmanship in applying the fasteners or adhesive. When clamping with several bar clamps, it is advised that the clamps be placed alternately one up and the next one down, thus preventing the surface from buckling. Clamps should be placed approximately 18 inches to 24 inches apart.

Edge Joints

Butt Joints (edge)

The butt joint is the most frequently used joint. It is constructed by butting together one member (end or edge) of wood to the end, edge, or surface of another. It is secured by using glue, nails, or screws. It is the weakest kind of joint, and should not be used where a great deal of pressure will be applied. The dowel, spline, or half-lap joint are recommended for edge joints.

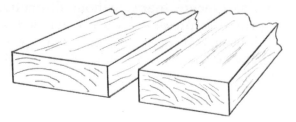

Dowel Joints (edge)

Dowels add strength to a butt joint. Drill holes for the dowel pins in the edges of the pieces of wood to be joined. For accuracy use a doweling jig. Apply glue to all parts, insert the dowels in one piece, continue to line up the other pieces, and join them together using clamps.

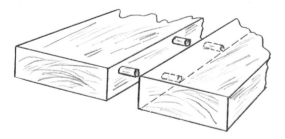

Spline Joints

The spline joint is made by cutting matching grooves or keyways into the edges of two boards. The spline is a narrow strip of thin wood made to fit the dimensions of the groove of both boards. The groove can be cut to any depth; the width is usually one–third the thickness of the stock. Cut the spline to fit into the grooves. Apply the glue to the parts to be joined. Install the splines into the matching grooves and fasten the boards together using clamps.

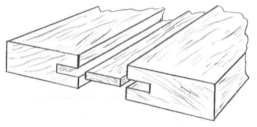

Rabbet or Half-Lap Joints (edge)

Two pieces of wood can be fastened together by using the rabbet or half-lap joint. The joint is made by cutting two rabbets one-half the thickness of the stock, hence a one–inch board will have a rabbet cut to one–half–inch thickness. When the two boards are fastened together with glue, they will equal a board one–inch thick.

Cut the rabbet joints to the necessary thickness; check them for proper fitness by fitting them together before gluing. Apply glue and clamp.

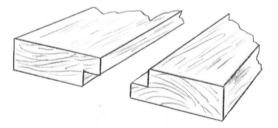

Tongue-and-Groove Joints

The tongue–and–groove joint is made by cutting two rabbets of equal dimensions on one board's edge to achieve the tongue, then by continuing to cut a groove to the width and depth of the tongue on the matching board. Fasten together by applying glue and clamps. The tongue and groove opening should not exceed half the thickness of the stock.

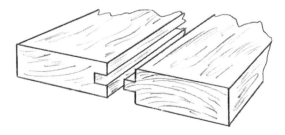

COMMON WOOD JOINTS

Butt Joints

The simple butt joint is the weakest joint used in assembling cut parts. The butt joint is constructed by butting one piece of wood to another at a right angle. The surface contact made is with the end grain of the wood. Because the end grain is extremely porous and may be difficult to glue, the butt joint should be reinforced with glue blocks screwed to the inside for added strength.

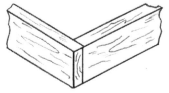

Dowel Joints

The dowel joint gives added strength to the butt joint by adding resistance to the cross strain of the stock. Drill holes for the dowel pins in the edges of the two pieces to be joined. Use a doweling jig for accuracy. Apply glue to the dowel pins and board edges. Insert the dowels in one piece, and continue to line up the piece. Join them together using clamps.

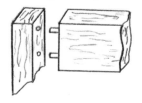

Miter Joints

A miter joint is a butt joint in which two pieces of stock are cut at the same angle, usually 45 degrees, in order to form a 90–degree angle. Because the joined surfaces are end grains, the joint is weak; it should be reinforced with a spline, dowels, or corrugated fasteners.

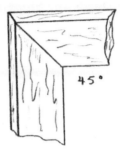

Half-Lap Joints

This joint has remarkable strength and is one of the most frequently used right–angled joints. It is constructed by cutting away half the thickness of each member to be joined so that when fastened together its thickness equals that of one member.

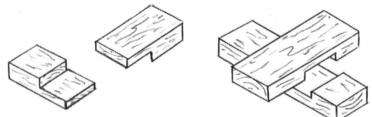

Rabbet Joints

A rabbet joint is a recess cut along the end or edge of a board. It is usually used in panel and drawer construction. The cut recess should be half to two-thirds the thickness of the stock. The rabbet joint should form a 90–degree angle.

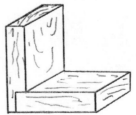

Dado Joints

A dado joint is often confused with a groove joint. A dado is a recess cut across the grain of wood into which another board is to fit. A groove is a recess cut with the grain of wood.

Dado and groove joints should never exceed more than one-half to two-thirds the thickness of the stock in which they are cut. The joint should fit snugly and the depth of the cut must be even.

Helpful Hint

The portable router operates at a very high speed (22,000 to 36,000 RPM) and is used by craftsmen for cutting woodworking joints, dadoes, rabbets, and dovetails. It is often used in free-hand cutting for various designs and for lettering signs. The router lends itself to creating a variety of edge molding designs for cuts on table tops, frames, and other woodcraft projects. The router is versatile, for it holds many different bits of shape and size. Each bit has two flutes, or cutting edges. The bits are available in high-speed steel or carbide-tipped cutting edges.

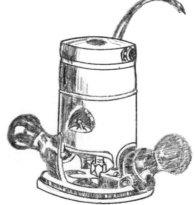

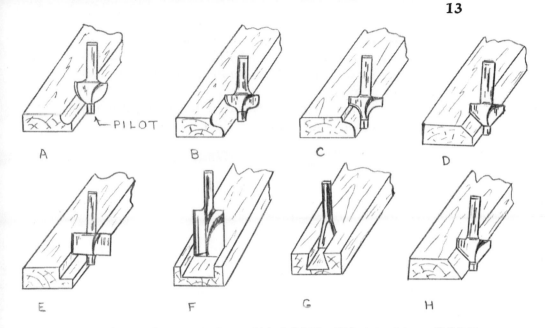

COMMON ROUTER CUTS: (A) COVE, (B) ROMAN OGEE, (G) QUATER ROUND, (D) CHAMFER, (E) RABBET, (F) STRAIGHT (G) DOVETAIL, (H) BEVEL.

CHAMFERING, BEVELING, AND TAPERING

The chamfer, bevel, and taper are three angled surfaces cut in the same manner. They are used to remove sharp corners from wood.

A *bevel* is an angled cut that is the full thickness of a piece of stock.

A *chamfer* is a slanted surface made by cutting off an end, edge, or corner of wood. The chamfered cut is made only part way down the edge of stock and is usually made to an angle of 45–degrees.

A *taper* is one or more cuts that become gradually smaller toward one end. Tapered cuts are often used for table and chair legs.

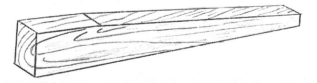

The tools necessary to lay out these three angled cuts are the sliding T-bevel, which is used to lay out and check any angle, and the protractor. The sliding T-bevel is a simple tool that consists of a blade and handle that has a locking screw to keep the blade in position. To adjust the T-bevel to a set position, use a metal or plastic protractor.

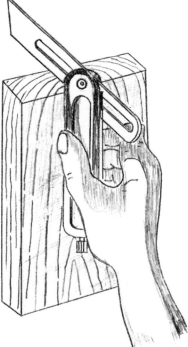

USING A SLIDING -T- BEVEL TO CHECK ANGLES.

Cutting a Chamfer

1. Locate and lay out the lines for the chamfer with a pencil.
2. Fasten the work into a vise. Make sure the chamfer is above the vise and facing toward you.
3. Begin to plane the chamfer by holding the plane at approximately a 45–degree angle.
4. When you have planed approximately two-thirds of the chamfer, check the chamfered cut. If there is an unequal amount to be planed, you may have to change the angle of the plane. Check the chamfer with the sliding T-bevel.

GUIDE LINES FOR CHAMFERING

PLANING CHAMFER

Cutting a Bevel

1. Decide on the angle of the bevel, then adjust the sliding T-bevel to the correct angle.
2. Locate and lay out the line across the ends of the stock to indicate the bevel angle. Continue to draw a line across the board surface of the stock as a guideline for planing.
3. Plane the bevel following the same procedure as when planing a chamfer. Be sure to check often with the sliding T-bevel to make sure you are planing at the correct angle.

Cutting Half–round Edges

If you wish to make a half–round edge on a board, it is first necessary to lay out lines with a pencil at approximately the center of the board's edge and on each opposite side (or face). Make sure the lines are an equal distance from the edge. Use the lines as a guide while shaping the half–round edge.

To begin shaping, use a jack or block plane adjusted for a light shaving to cut the regular chamfers on both faces of the board. Bring the chamfers to a crude rounding by making a series of fine cuts in a graduated manner until the edge is roughly rounded. To bring the edge to its final smooth half–round shape, continue to use a half–round wood file for shaping; then sand the edge smooth.

CHAMFER CUT ON TOP AND BOTTOM EDGES FOR HALF ROUNDING

FILING AND SANDING TO FINAL SHAPE

Cutting Edge Molding

1. Select the cutter of your choice. Some router bits are equipped with a pilot to limit the depth of the cut.
2. Lock the bit in the chuck and adjust the base to the desired height. If the bit has no pilot, the straight guide must be fastened to the router base

and be properly adjusted to the correct depth of the cut.

3. Start the router and move it slowly over the stock from left to right. Be sure to hold the base firmly against the surface to firmly maintain an even cut. Make sure the straight guide or the pilot guide is in firm contact with the edge at all times.

4. If a router bit with a pilot is used, make sure an excessive amount of pressure is not exerted against the edge of the board; too much pressure will result in burning the edge. Burning is also a result of using a dull cutter bit.

Cutting a Dado or a Rabbet

1. Select a straight router bit of the correct size, and fasten it in the collet.

2. Adjust the base to the correct depth of cut desired.

3. Attach the straight guide to the router base, then proceed to adjust it to give the desired width of cut.

4. The wood stock to be cut should be securely fastened to a bench top.

5. Start the router and slowly move it over the stock from left to right (this is the direction of the cut). Make sure the base is held flat against the stock and the straight guide is firm against the edge.

6. If the rabbet cut is wider than the diameter of the cutter bit, the cut can be made wider by moving the straight guide in or out.

7. Dadoes and grooves are cut following the same procedure as above. If the dado is to be cut out of the reach of the straight guide, a small board can be clamped to the stock to serve as a straight–edge rub-guide.

WOOD FASTENERS
Nails and Corrugated Fasteners

The kinds of nails most often used in woodworking are *box nails*. They are relatively thin and have flat heads. Since they are made of a relatively small wire gauge, they may be used to nail thin stock. They were first made for nailing together boxes built of thin wood which split easily.

Common nails have heavy, flat heads and are used where more holding power is desired. The wire gauge of the common nail is heavier than the gauge of the box nail.

Finishing nails have small heads. They can be set with a nail set and covered with plastic wood or stick shellac. The finishing nail has a smaller gauge wire than the common nail and will not split the wood.

Casing nails are similar to finishing nails but have a larger cone-shaped head, which gives them more holding power than the finishing nail. They are used mostly for interior trim and cabinet work.

The *brad* is a small finishing nail. It varies in length from ¼ inch to 1¼ inches, and is used to nail thin stock together.

The size of nails is indicated by the term *penny* or its abbreviation, D. The nail chart shows the sizes and lengths of nails. A 2-penny (2-D) nail is one inch long.

For each additional penny add ¼ inch in length up to three inches. For example, a 10-penny (10-D) is three inches long.

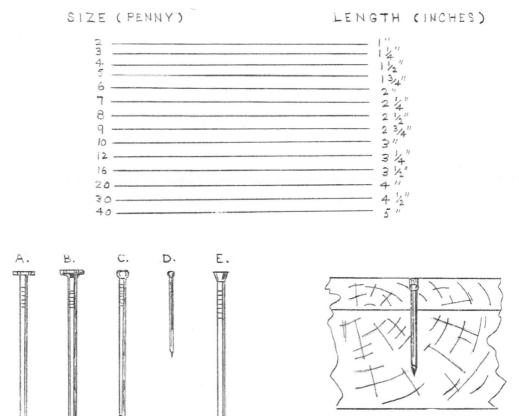

SIZE (PENNY)   LENGTH (INCHES)

2	1"
3	1 1/4"
4	1 1/2"
5	1 3/4"
6	2"
7	2 1/4"
8	2 1/2"
9	2 3/4"
10	3"
12	3 1/4"
16	3 1/2"
20	4"
30	4 1/2"
40	5"

A. B. C. D. E.

A. BOX   C. FINISH   E. CASING   FINISH NAIL SET AND FILLED
B. COMMON   D. BRAD

Corrugated fasteners are used to hold mitered or butt joints together. They may be used in simple frame construction where it is necessary to assemble parts quickly. They are also used to add strength to glued joints. Clamps are often used to hold parts of frames tightly together while driving in a corrugated fastener.

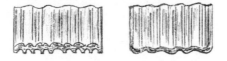

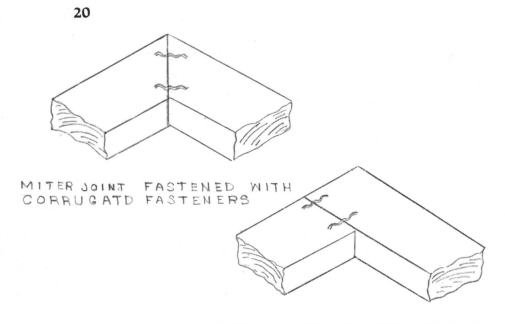

MITER JOINT FASTENED WITH CORRUGATD FASTENERS

BUTT JOINT FASTENED WITH CORRUGATED FASTENERS

Tools for Nailing

The *claw hammer* is the most popular hammer in use. The size is reckoned by the weight of the hammer head. The most common sizes are 14 and 16 ounces. The claw may be straight or curved.

The *nail set* is used to recess the heads of brads, finishing, and casing nails below the surface of the wood. The tip of the nail set is concave, which prevents it from sliding off the nail head. Nail sets can be purchased in various sizes.

Helpful Hints

1. Try to drive the nail in at a slight angle. Tests prove that nails driven in this way have more holding power.
2. If nails are to be driven in close to the end or edge of such hardwoods as oak, birch, maple and others, it is wise to drill small pilot holes where the nails are to be driven in. This will prevent splitting the wood.
3. The length of nail used should be two-and-a-half to three times the thickness of the first board the nail goes through.

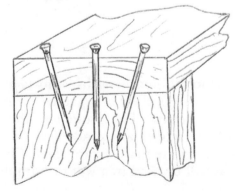

Wood Screws

Wood screws are often used to assemble a craft project. The advantages of using screws are that a project can be taken apart easily and reassembled and that screws are a superior fastener, for they hold better than nails and may be tightened easily.

The most common types of screws are the *round-head, flat-head* and *oval-head*. The flat-head and round-head are used most often in woodworking. Most screws have a plain slotted head. However, the *Phillips-head* screw has become popular due to its neater appearance and stronger head.

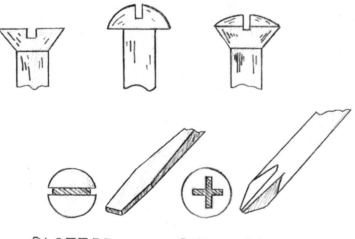

SLOTTED   PHILLIPS

Screws come in different lengths from $\frac{1}{4}$ inch to six inches. In gauge (sizes) they are graded from 0, the smallest, to 24, the largest. The gauge tells the diameter of the shank. Most screws are made from mild steel. However, some screws are made from brass. They are used for items that will be used in a wet or humid environment.

Screws are sold by the dozen or by the gross (144). Boxes of screws are labeled to show the length, type, and the material and diameter of the shank (gauge).

Fastening Boards With Screws

1. Mark the location for the screw hole with a scratch awl or nail point.
2. Select the drill bit that is the correct size to accommodate the shank of the screw.
3. Position the point of the bit on the center mark and drill the shank hole. Be careful to keep the bit at a 90–degree angle to the surface being drilled.
4. Position and drill all other shank holes.
5. Position boards that are to be joined. Lay out the location of the pilot hole with a scratch awl.
6. Drill the pilot hole with a drill bit diameter equal to the core of the screw.
7. Countersink the shank hole if a flat head or oval head is to be used.
8. Counterbore the shank hole if the screw is to be concealed with a furniture button or dowel plug. To counterbore means to set (sink) the head in the wood.

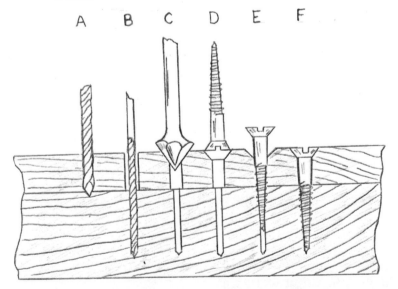

PROCEDURES IN-INTSALLING FLAT-HEAD SCREWS (A) DRILL THE SHANK HOLE. (B) DRILL THE PILOT HOLE. (C) COUNTERSINK. (D) CHECK SIZE OF COUNTERSINK WITH THE HEAD OF A SCREW. (E) FASTEN FLAT-HEAD SCREW. (F) SCREW CORRECTLY FASTENED.

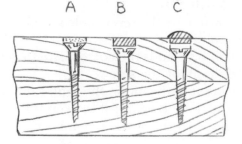

METHODS OF CONCEALING
FLAT-HEAD SCREWS. FIRST
COUNTERBORE OVER THE
SHANK HOLE THEN FILL WITH
(A) PLASTIC WOOD (B) DOWEL PLUG
(C) FURNITURE BUTTON.

9. Select a screwdriver which fits the slot of the screw snugly. Turn the screw in a clockwise direction until the pieces of stock are drawn together tightly.
10. After the final screw has been installed, test all other screws to see that they are tight.

The screw eye is used for hooks on doors, hanging mirrors, picture frames, and planters, and in other places as an anchor for small objects to be hung. The cup-hook, screw-hook and L-screw hook are used mainly to hang articles. These special wood screws can be obtained in various amounts in a variety of stores.

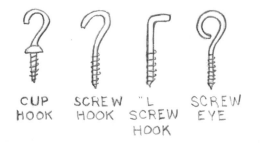

CUP HOOK   SCREW HOOK   "L SCREW HOOK   SCREW EYE

Hinges and Other Hardware

Hardware is part of the final trim used in many projects. It is important to select the proper style of hardware for a specific piece. For example, a pair of Early American hinges would not look proper on a modern chest. Hardware stores and craft supply shops carry a wide selection of items. It is wise to select hardware carefully; have an idea of what you want before you go to the store.

Some of the more common pieces of hardware are:

Hinges

The *butt hinge* is most common. It requires layout and gaining (chiseling out) of the cabinet or frame so that both leaves of the hinge can be recessed into the wood. Butt hinges can be purchased with loose or stationary pins. If the pin is loose, the hinge should be installed with the head of the pin up so that the pin will not fall out.

BUTT HINGE   ANTIQUE BUTT HINGE

The *surface hinge,* as the name suggests, is designed to fit on the face of a flat surface. It is the easiest to install and can be purchased in many different styles, such as traditional, modern, and Early American.

Invisible hinges are mostly used in pieces of fine furniture where it is desired that the hinges be concealed. It is important to read the manufacturer's directions with accuracy before installation.

The *chest hinge* is often used to hinge chest lids in place. The *combination hinge* is also used for this purpose since it also has a built-in lid support and stop.

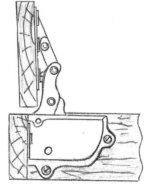

Offset hinges are installed with the lip or rabbeted edge down. When fastened in place properly, only the joints of the hinges are visible.

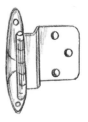

Chest or Drawer Locks

The chest or drawer lock is installed on the inside surface of a woodcraft project by boring a hole through the stock to accommodate the diameter of the barrel of the lock.

Drawer Knobs and Handles

These are made in a wide selection of designs. It is possible to find an attractive knob or handle to meet your needs. They range from brass handles for modern projects to Early American for colonial projects. Knobs and handles are sold with the screws necessary for installation.

Installing a Butt Hinge

1. A lid or door is hung with two or three hinges; therefore, it is wise to select the size and number of hinges according to the size of the lid or door being hung.
2. Place the lid or door in the opening. If hanging a door, place a small wedge at the bottom right side of the door.
3. Measure and mark the location of the hinges ac-

cording to the working drawing. The marks should be located on both the door and the frame.

4. Lay out the depth and width of the gain (a notch cut out with a chisel). Use a marking gauge.
5. Hold the chisel in a vertical position on the line which locates the ends of the hinge, then continue to drive the chisel moderately with a mallet.
6. Being careful not to split the wood, continue the chisel–cutting on the line which follows in the direction of the grain.
7. Make a series of chisel relief cuts as shown in the drawing.

CHISELING A GAIN FOR A BUTT HINGE

8. Trim the bottom of the gain with a wide chisel.
9. Check to see if the hinge fits in the gain; if not, trim where necessary to make a snug fit.
10. Locate the hinge in position. Lay out the holes for

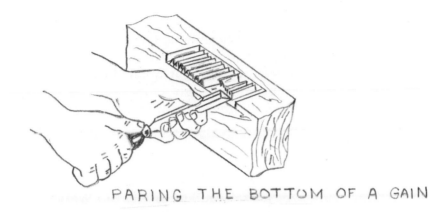

PARING THE BOTTOM OF A GAIN

the screws with an awl or pencil.
11. Locate and drill pilot holes into the wood.
12. With a screw driver install the screws until the hinges are fastened securely.
13. Finish cutting the remaining gains.

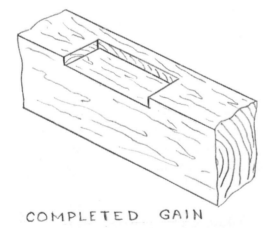

COMPLETED GAIN

14. Attach the door or lid into its correct position.
15. Check to see if the door or lid operates correctly; if it does, make sure all screws are tight.

GLUING

The variety of glues available to the consumer seems to be almost endless. Today, the most commonly used glues are:

Polyvinyl Acetate (PVA)

An excellent glue for most household projects including ceramic work, craftwork, and furniture construction. PVA glue will give an excellent bond, but cannot withstand excessive moisture or high temperature. PVA should set for at least 8 hours in a 65-/to 0-degree Farenheit temperature.

Polyvinyl Chloride (PVC)

An excellent waterproof adhesive for use on wood, metal, china, glass, or porcelain. The drying time varies, and brand specifications should therefore be noted.

Cellulose Glue

Best suited for small repairs to furniture and model work. Cellulose is superior for joining chinaware and glass. It also can be used on most fabrics. It yields a fast–drying, colorless joint. The bond strength is increased by applying two coats to both surfaces.

Epoxy Glue

Excellent for joining glass and metals as well as for china repairs. It is waterproof and oil resistant. Epoxy glues are excellent for bonding dissimilar materials, such as plastic to metal, glass to metal, and glass to concrete. They are available in regular and fastsetting types, and consist of a resin and a hardener that are to be mixed in equal amounts.

Liquid Hide Glue

The traditional glue of cabinetmakers. It is best suited for furniture repair and construction. Hide glue makes an excellent bond and can withstand a heavy load. Do not use hide glue on projects that will be exposed to water or high humidity.

Joint preparation is extremely important because dirt or oil or even a fine film of dust will prevent a good bond. To bond wood joints, be certain the surfaces are square and sanded properly; all sanding dust must be cleaned off the surfaces before applying the glue.

It is important that joints are fitted tightly, and should be held secure with bar clamps, screw clamps, or spring clamps. Repairs made to china, glass, and plastic can be clamped with makeshift devices, such as small jigs, masking tape, and elastic bands.

If a wood joint is loose, it can be tightened by filling the space with a small wood sliver. Cut the slivers to the size needed, then apply the glue. Press the sliver into the gap. For smaller jobs use crack fillers such as plastic wood

FINISHING THE PROJECT

It is crucial that the project be carefully sanded to a smooth surface before the application of a finish. Although power sanders may help to do much of the sanding, only careful hand-sanding can bring professional results. It is foolish to think that stain or paint will conceal a poorly prepared surface.

Sanding of the project should be done in stages starting with 60 to 80 grit paper for rough work, then continuing with 120 to 150 grit paper for smoothing. To produce a smoother surface, use 220 to 280 grit paper. It is good practice to do all sanding in a straight line moving with the grain of the wood.

Splits, checks, or nail holes should be filled with plastic wood or stick shellac. These products can be purchased in a multitude of colors to match the color of your wood or stain.

A finish should not be applied in extremely damp or cold weather.

When staining, do in a spot that has the same amount of light that the project will receive when in use. receive in use.

The purpose of stain is twofold: to emphasize the beauty of the grain, and to color the wood to your liking.

STAINING

There are several types of stains: oil stains and dye stains being the most common. These are applied in liquid form and require varying amounts of drying time. When the stain has been thoroughly dried, the surface should be given several coats of clear varnish, linseed oil, or lacquer for protection.

Oil Stains

These are composed of finely ground powders mixed to a paste with benzene or turpentine. These stains can be applied with a rag or brush. The stain can be rubbed on in any direction and should be given 15 to 20 minutes to dry. It should then be rubbed off in the direction of the grain with a clean cloth. If the color tone is too light, allow the first coat to dry overnight; then apply a second coat.

Dye Stains

These normally have a water or alcohol base. They soak into wood very fast, and should, therefore, be treated with very light coats. Dye stains are known for their rich quality of color and the manner in which they bring out the grain characteristics of wood. Dye stains must be mixed since they come in powdered form. The powder is mixed with hot water. The advantage of mixing your own stain is that if your color is too light you can darken it by adding more powder, and dark colors can be lightened by adding more water. Two coats of stain should be applied to yield the best results.

One disadvantage of using a water base stain is that it raises the grain of the wood. To remedy this allow it to dry overnight, then sand the surface lightly with 280 grit sandpaper.

Alcohol base stains have the advantage of not raising the grain of wood. Since they are sold premixed in a variety of colors, the intensity of their colors can be reduced by adding alcohol.

Dye stains can be applied to the wood by wiping with a rag, spraying, or by using a brush. Always be careful to (1) wear gloves when applying, (2) not work near an open flame or in a very hot room, and (3) not smoke while applying the stain.

Varnish

There are many grades and colors of varnish available; they are sold ready to use. The better grades will expand and contract with the wood to which they are applied without cracking. The colors range from clear to dark brown. Varnish will dry to a scratch-resistant surface that is hard enough to rub down between applications.

Cellulose (better known as polyurethane) varnish is extremely durable and is unaffected by water. It does not discolor when exposed to light.

Spar varnish is a variety that has been treated with chemicals to make it resistant to salt water.

Turpentine acts as a suitable thinner and cleaning agent for all varnishes.

When applying varnish to bare wood, the pores should be filled and the surface made as dust-free as possible. At least two coats of varnish should be applied, and the rubbing between each coat done with fine steel wool or extra fine sandpaper. As you rub between coats, you will feel the varnish becoming smooth as the bubbles and dust particles disappear. It is wise to allow plenty of drying time for a hard finish coat, for the harder the surface becomes the easier it is to rub down the coats.

Varnish is sold as high gloss, satin finish, or flat finish. Your selection will depend on the finish you would like to achieve.

Lacquer

Lacquer is an excellent finish, for it tends to dry fast and does not conceal the wood color. It can be identified faster than other finishes because of its banana-like odor.

Lacquers are available to be brushed on or sprayed. Lacquer that is brushed on takes longer to dry than sprayed lacquer. Brush–type lacquer has a heavier consistency than the spray–type and therefore requires a longer drying period. When thin coats are applied, the drying time is always reduced.

Once the work is sanded to a smooth surface and stained, apply the first coat of lacquer by brushing or spraying. A good spray job should have at least three to four light coats. Rubbing between each coat is not essential because lacquer tends to settle into a smooth surface.

Care must be taken in using a spray gun because heavy spraying has a tendency to run, and it is almost impossible to lift the heavy runs of lacquer. Lacquer should be thinned with lacquer thinner *only*.

To brush on the lacquer, apply the first coat as evenly as possible in the direction of the wood grain. After an overnight drying period, apply the second coat. After the final application has dried for 36 hours, some imperfections may appear because of dust particles and small pits. These can be taken out easily by rubbing the surface down with wax imbedded into the steel wool pad. All safety rules for applying a combustible finish should be followed carefully when working with lacquer.

Finishing Oil

Applying oil to wood is one of the oldest and best known methods of wood finishing. It is easy to apply and to maintain. A wood surface finished with oil will tend to dry out in time and can be easily revived with one new application of oil. If the surface is dirty, all that is required is to wipe it down with turpentine or rub the dirt spots with steel wool.

Linseed oil is probably the best type of oil finish, for it tends to last longest. When working with linseed oil, one should use boiled linseed oil diluted with one part of turpentine for each part linseed oil. Also, the formula may be adjusted to your individual taste.

The project should be sanded to a smooth surface, with dust thoroughly removed. Wipe or brush the oil on generously with a clean cloth. Allow the oil to saturate the wood, and if dull spots appear, add more oil. When the wood can absorb no more oil, wipe off the excess with a clean cloth. Rub the surface down with a lint-free cloth folded into a pad. This will produce a satin finish. The key to working with oil is that one must rub hard enough with the heel of his hand to produce heat.After drying for 24 hours, repeat the same procedure 4 to 6 times to produce a beautiful satin finish.

Pumice

Pumice is a light, porous material obtained from volcanic lava. It acts as a sharp cutting material which smooths and polishes by producing fine, hairlike scratches. Pumice is available in powdered form and is used with oil, water, or paraffin to produce a smooth surface.

A light film of oil or lubricant is applied to a cloth pad with pumice sprinkled over it. Rub the pumice in the direction of the grain until you reach a smooth finished surface.

Wax

Paste wax adds protection and life to a finished surface by covering it with a tough film. The film protects the surface by making it water-repellent and abrasion-resistant.

Some waxes require a damp cloth as an applicator. When applying the wax, one should work in an area of approximately three square feet at a time. The paste should be applied in an even layer. After its recommended drying time, it should be buffed thoroughly. Polish the adjacent area, making sure to blend the entire finish so there are no bare spots.

USING THE PLANS

As you look through this book, you will notice that most of the drawings are *working*, or *view*, drawings. There are one, two, or three views of each project. The

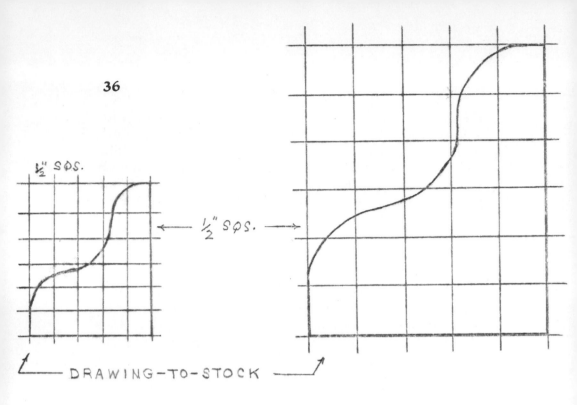

$\frac{1}{2}''$ SQS.

←——— $\frac{1}{2}''$ SQS. ———→

∠——— DRAWING-TO-STOCK ———↗

most typical views are from the front, tip, and end. Some of the project drawings in this book are pictorial drawings. The pictorial drawing shows how the project will look when fully constructed; it also shows the size and shape of each drawing.

Before starting a woodworking craft project, it is important to study the working drawing which specifies the size and shape of all parts. It will help you in many ways and will serve as your blueprint. It will guide you, for example, in achieving the shape of curved and scrolled parts.

In order to reproduce the design on your wood, merely lay out the required grid or squares on the stock, then draw the suggested shape square by square (see illustration).

A suggested list of materials is given for each woodworking craft project in this book. Dimensions are given for each piece to be used for the project, along with the hardware needed.

CHANDELIER

1

Materials Required

Part	Number	Size	Material
center piece	1	3½ " x 3½ " x 7½ "	walnut
candle holders	8	2" x 2" x 4"	walnut
dowels	8	⅜" x 14"	birch
shaker knob	2	1¾ " diameter	birch
shaker knob	8	1¼ " diameter	birch
eye hook	1	¾ "	

Note: As an alternative to the shaker knobs, use brass or porcelain knobs. These can be purchased at a local hardware store.

Chandelier Plans

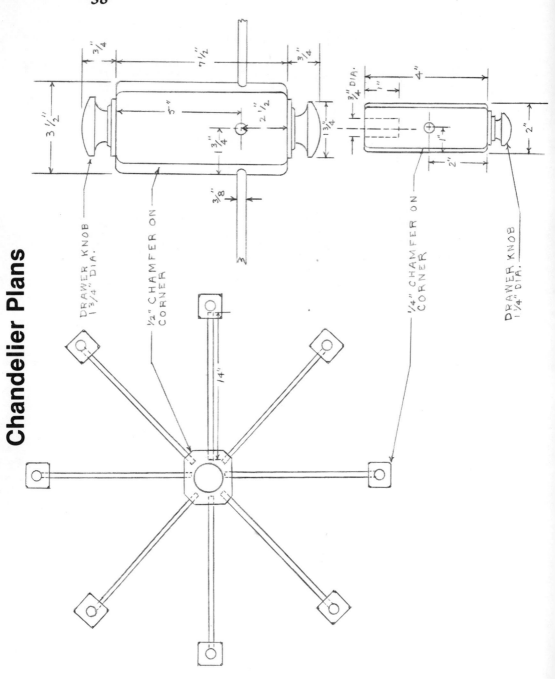

DRAWER KNOB 1 3/4" DIA.

1/2" CHAMFER ON CORNER

3/4"

7 1/2"

3/4"

3 1/2"

5"

2 1/2"

1 3/4"

1 3/4"

3/8"

3/4" DIA.

1"

4"

2"

1"

2"

1/4" CHAMFER ON CORNER

DRAWER KNOB 1 1/4" DIA.

14"

Procedure

1. Lay out and cut all stock to the suggested size.
2. Lay out and cut the four ½-inch chamfer designs on the center piece. Continue to lay out and cut the four chamfered designs on the eight candle holder blocks.
3. Position and bore the eight ⅜-inch diameter holes into the center piece to a depth of ¾ of an inch. Be sure that all holes are aligned. Position and bore the eight ⅜-inch holes into the eight candle holders to a depth of ¾ of an inch.
4. Fasten the correct knobs to the center piece and candle holders by gluing and clamping. If the knobs have a tenon, bore the correct hole; then fasten with glue.
5. Fasten all the dowels with glue into the holes in the center piece and candle holders. Be sure that the candle holders are straight.
6. Clean all traces of glue and proceed to sand the project to a smooth surface. Since this project is made of hardwood, a clear stain is best suited. Apply several coats of finishing oil, rubbing lightly between each coat with fine steel wool or pumice and oil. To protect the finish use paste wax and buff.
7. Attach the ¾-inch eye hook to the top of the walnut center piece.

WOODEN LANTERN

2

Materials Required

Part	Number	Size	Material
side	4	½" x 7" x 10"	cherry or the wood of your choice
top	1	½" x 6" x 6"	
bottom	1	½" x 6" x 6"	
handle	one piece of	⅛" x ½" x 12"	band iron
glue			
screws	2	#6 round head, ¾" black finish	

Wooden Lantern Plans

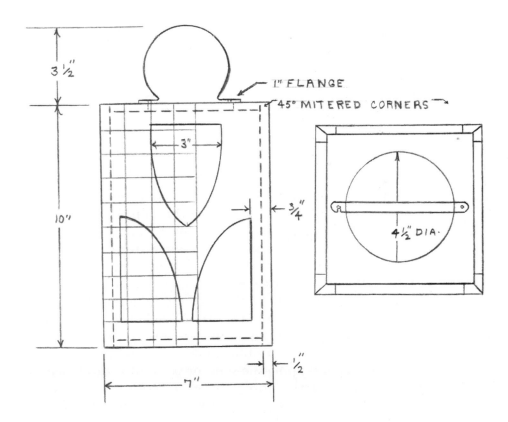

3 ½"

1" FLANGE

45° MITERED CORNERS

3"

10"

¾"

4 ½" DIA.

½"

7"

WOODEN LANTERN

Procedure

1. Lay out and cut the four sides to the suggested size and design. To cut out the designs, first drill a $3/8$-inch hole through each shape, then insert the blade of a sabre saw or jig saw.

2. Set the saw to a 45–degree angle, then cut each side piece to construct the miter joints. Fasten the four side pieces together using glue and 1–inch finishing brads. If you do not wish to use the miter joint for the corners, the simple butt joint or rabbet joint will suffice.

3. Lay out and cut the top and bottom pieces to the size indicated. Fasten the top and bottom pieces to the sides by gluing and clamping.

4. Locate the center of the top and lay out a $4\frac{1}{2}$–inch diameter hole. Cut out the piece by drilling a $3/8$-inch hole, then inserting a sabre saw blade.

5. Shape the handle by bending a $1/8''$ x $\frac{1}{2}''$ x 12-inch piece of band iron around a 1 inch x $3\frac{1}{2}$–inch diameter wood disk. At approximately 1 inch from each end, bend the band iron to form a flange. Drill a $3/16$–inch hole through the center of each flanged end. Attach the handle to the top with two -6, $3/4$–inch black round head screws. If the handle is to pivot, open cut into one $3/16$–inch hole with a hack saw.

6. Scrape all traces of glue, set and fill all holes, then sand to a smooth surface. Added design can be achieved by using a file or router to create a chamfered cut around each cutout shape.

7. Select and apply the stain or paint of your choice. When dry, apply several coats of clear polyurethane finish, rubbing between coats with fine steel wool or pumice and oil. Protect the finish with paste wax and buff.

Note: The band iron handle should be painted with flat black.

CHEST

3

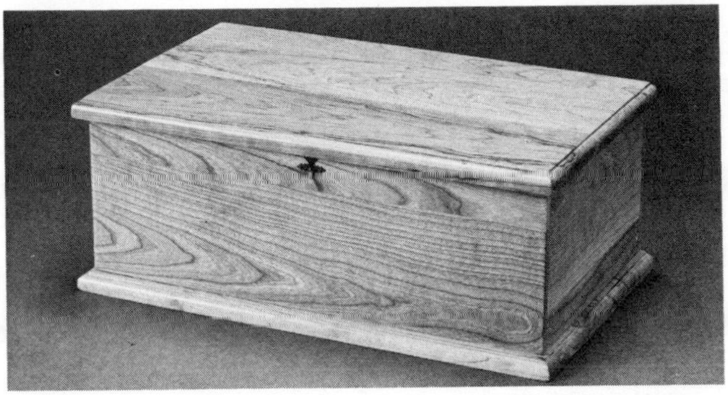

Materials Required

Part	*Number*	*Size*	*Material*
top	1	¾ ″ x 13″ x 22″	pine or the wood of your choice
base	1	¾ ″ x 13″ x 22″	
side	2	¾ ″ x 7″ x 20¾ ″	
butt hinge	2	⅛″ x ¾ ″	
nails		#6 finishing	
glue			

Chest Plans

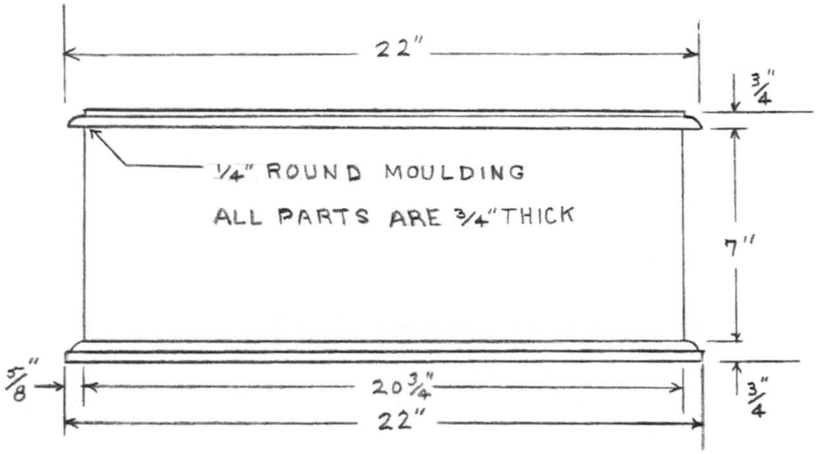

22″
¾″
¼″ ROUND MOULDING
ALL PARTS ARE ¾″ THICK
7″
⅝″
20¾″
22″
¾″

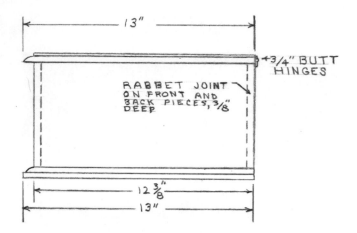

Procedure

1. Glue up and clamp the stock to the required width, then lay out and cut the pieces to the suggested size.
2. With a router and quarter round bit cut the design around the top and base pieces.
3. Lay out and cut the ⅜ x ¾–inch rabbet joints on the front and back pieces.
4. Assemble the sides together by gluing and clamping. Fasten the base to the box assembly with glue and #6 finishing nails.
5. Locate and fasten the two ¾–inch butt hinges approximately 2 inches from each end.
6. Scrape all traces of glue, set and fill all nail holes, then sand the chest to a smooth surface.
7. Select and apply the stain or paint of your choice. When dry, apply several coats of clear lacquer finish, rubbing between coats with fine steel wool or pumice and lemon oil. To protect the finish, apply a coat of paste wax and buff.

HAND MIRROR

4

Materials Required

Part	Number	Size	Material
wood frame	1	⅜" x 4¼" x 11"	cherry, walnut, or the hard wood of your choice
oval mirror	1	⅛" x 3½" x 5½" oval	
epoxy			

Note: The oval mirror pattern can be cut to size at your local glass dealer, or it can be purchased pre-cut from your local craft supply store.

Hand Mirror Plans

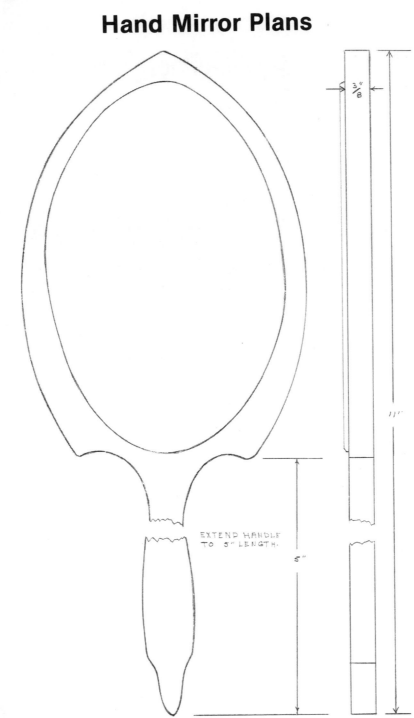

EXTEND HANDLE
TO 5" LENGTH.

5"

3"/8

11"

Procedure

1. Lay out and cut the full size pattern on the wood of your choice.
2. With a half–round file round the edges of the mirror.
3. Sand the project to a smooth surface.
4. Apply several coats of clear oil finish, rubbing between coats with fine steel wool or pumice and oil.
5. When the finish is thoroughly dry, fasten the oval mirror with epoxy glue spread evenly on the back of the oval mirror. Use a spring clamp to hold the oval mirror in place. Care should be taken to avoid spreading glue on any exposed wood surface.

SERVING TRAY

5

Materials Required

Part	Number	Size	Material
base	1	½ " x 10¼ " x 17 "	pine
side	2	⅜ " x ¾ " x 17 "	walnut
handle	2	¼ " x 2½ " x 10 "	walnut

Serving Tray Plans

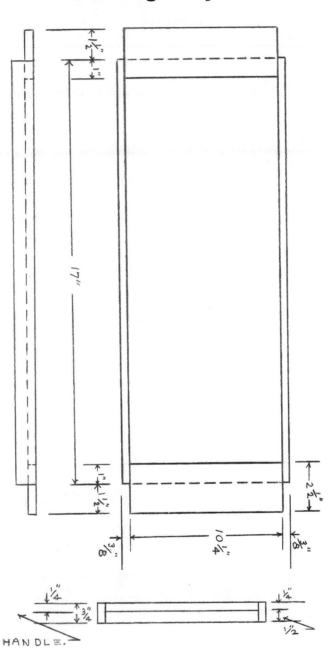

HANDLE.

SERVING TRAY

Procedure

1. Glue up and clamp enough stock to achieve the required width.
2. Lay out and cut all of the pieces to the size indicated.
3. Fasten the two ⅜ x ¾ x 17–inch strips to the sides of the base by gluing and clamping.
4. Fasten the two handles onto the ends of the base by gluing and clamping; allow the handles to extend out 1½ inches.
5. Scrape all traces of glue, then sand the tray to a smooth surface.
6. Apply several coats of clear finishing oil, rubbing between coats with fine steel wool or pumice and lemon oil. Protect the finish by applying a coat of paste wax and buffing.

STEP STOOL

6

Materials Required

Part	Number	Size	Material
top	1	¾ " x 8½ " x 16 "	cherry or the wood of your choice
side	2	¾ " x 13½ " x 10¾ "	
step shelf	1	¾ " x 12½ " x 14¼ "	
front	1	¾ " x 5½ " x 13½ "	
back	1	¾ " x 2 " x 13½ "	
nails		#6 finishing	
glue			
wood screws		#10, 1½ ", flathead	
dowel plugs			
(or furniture buttons)		⅜ "	

Step Stool Plans

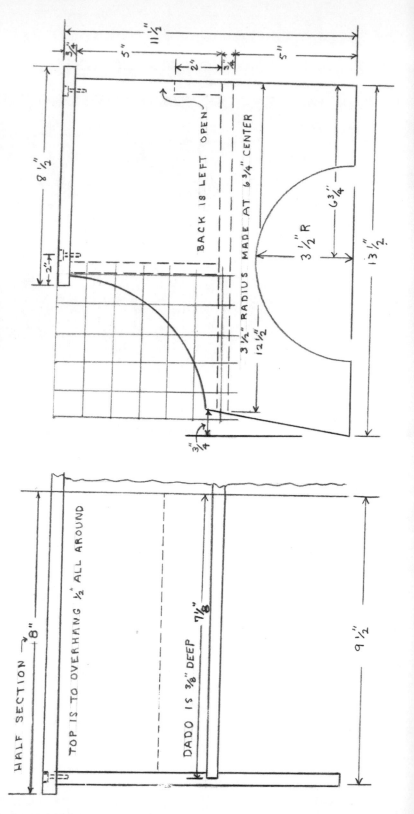

11 1/2"

3/4"

5"

2"

3/4"

5"

8 1/2"

BACK IS LEFT OPEN

3 3/4" RADIUS MADE AT 6 3/4" CENTER

2"

3 1/2" RADIUS

12 1/2"

6 3/4"

3 1/2" R

13 1/2"

3/4"

HALF SECTION

8"

TOP IS TO OVERHANG 1/2" ALL AROUND

DADO IS 3/8" DEEP

7 1/2"

9 1/2"

Procedure

1. Lay out and cut all pieces to the suggested size and shape.
2. Lay out and cut the two ⅜ x ¾–inch dado joints, then fasten the step shelf to the side pieces with glue and #6 finishing nails.
3. Fasten the front and back pieces to the sides then locate and drill four ⅜–inch counterbored pilot holes through the top and into the side pieces. Attach the top to the assembly with #10, 1½–inch flathead wood screws. Fill the counterbored holes with ⅜–inch dowel plugs or ⅜–inch furniture buttons.
4. Scrape all traces of glue, set and fill all nail holes, then sand the stool to a smooth surface.
5. Select and apply the stain or paint of your choice. When dry, apply several coats of clear polyurethane finish, rubbing between coats with fine steel wool or pumice and oil. Protect the finish by applying a coat of paste wax and buffing.

SCONCE WITH DRAWER

7

Materials Required

Part	Number	Size	Material
back	1	½ " x 7" x 14½ "	cherry or the wood of your choice
side	2	½ " x 4½ " x 7½ "	
shelf	1	½ " x 4⅜ " x 6"	
Drawer parts:			
front	1	⅜ " x 3 " x 5⅞ "	
side	2	⅜ " x 2⅞ " x 3⅞ "	
back	1	⅜ " x 2⅞ " x 5⅛ "	
bottom	1	⅜ " x 2⅞ " x 3¼ "	
candle cup	1	optional sizes and designs	
mirror	1	oval ⅛ "	
nails		#4 finishing	
brads		1 " finishing	
glue			
glass points			

Sconce With Drawer Plans

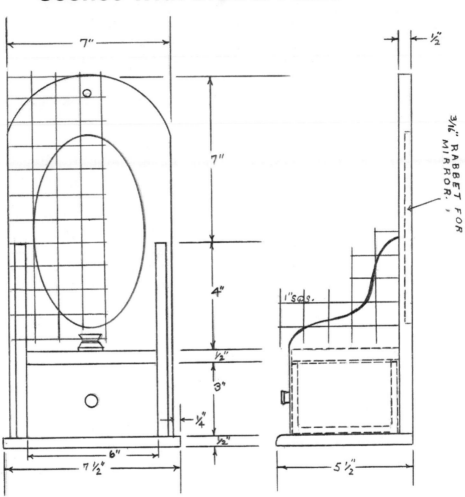

7"

7"

4"

½"

3"

¼"

½"

6"

7 ½"

½

3/16" RABBET FOR MIRROR.

1"SQS.

5 ½"

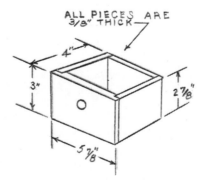

ALL PIECES ARE
3/8" THICK

4"

3"

2 ⅞"

5 ⅞"

Procedure

1. Lay out and cut all pieces to the suggested size and shape.
2. Cut a $\frac{3}{16}$ x $\frac{3}{8}$–inch rabbet cut on the back side of the oval frame. The recess can be cut by using a router and rabbet bit.
3. Fasten the sides to the back with glue and #4 finishing nails. Attach the bottom and shelf using glue and #4 finishing nails.
4. Cut a $\frac{3}{16}$ x $\frac{3}{8}$–inch rabbet joint into the front piece of the drawer, then proceed to assemble the drawer using glue and 1–inch finishing brads.
5. Fasten the optional candle cup to the shelf by gluing and clamping or by drilling and screwing.
6. To hang the sconce drill a $\frac{3}{16}$–inch diameter hole.
7. Clean all traces of glue, set and fill all holes, then proceed to sand the sconce to a smooth surface.
8. Select and apply the colored stain or paint of your choice. When dry, apply several coats of clear lacquer or polyurethane finish, rubbing lightly between each coat. To protect the surface apply a coat of paste wax and buff.
9. Fasten the oval mirror into the recess by tacking in glass points approximately five inches apart.
10. Find the center of the drawer then drill and fasten a $\frac{1}{2}$–inch porcelain knob.

SCONCE WITH MIRROR

8

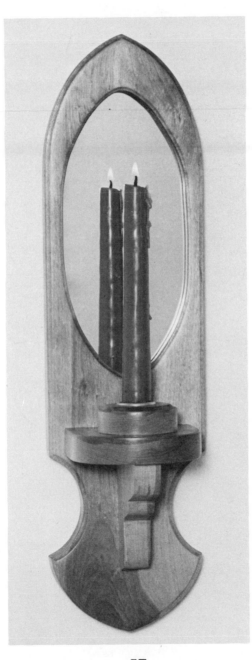

Materials Required

Part	Number	Size	Material
back	1	¼″ x 5″ x 18″	cherry or the wood of your choice
bracket	1	¾″ x 3″ x 3″	
shelf	1	¾″ x 4″ x 4″	
disk	1	¾″ x 2³⁄₁₆″ dia.	
candle cup			
wood screws	2	#9, 1½″, flathead	
glue			
mirror	1	⅛″	

Note: The oval mirror can be purchased pre-cut from a craft shop or it can be cut to the pattern at your local glass dealer.

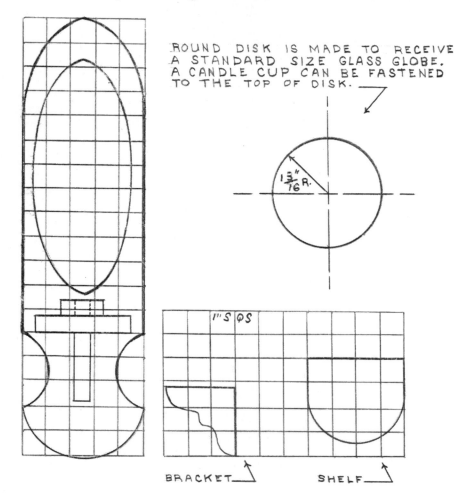

ROUND DISK IS MADE TO RECEIVE A STANDARD SIZE GLASS GLOBE. A CANDLE CUP CAN BE FASTENED TO THE TOP OF DISK.

$1\frac{3}{16}$″ R.

1″ SQS

BRACKET

SHELF

Procedure

1. Lay out and cut all pieces to the suggested size and design.
2. Use a router and rabbet bit to cut a $\frac{1}{4}$ x $\frac{3}{8}$–inch rabbet recess on the back side of the oval. The cut is made to set in the oval mirror.
3. If the disk is to be used to hold the candle, bore a $\frac{3}{4}$–inch diameter hole through the center. An option can be to attach a candle cup to the center of the disk.
4. Glue and clamp the disk to the center of the shelf, then glue and clamp the bracket to the bottom of the shelf.
5. Fasten the bracket to the back piece by drilling two pilot and countersunk holes, then screwing through the back and into the bracket.
6. Round the edges of the sconce with a half–round file to a smooth surface.
7. Select and apply the colored stain or paint of your choice. When dry, apply several coats of clear polyurethane finish. Rub between each coat with fine steel wool or pumice and oil. Protect the finish by applying a coat of paste wax and buffing.
8. Fasten the oval mirror into the rabbet recess with glass points placed 3 inches apart.

CHECKER / CHESS BOARD

9

Materials Required

Part	Number	Size	Material
strip	5	1″ x 1½″ x 13″	maple
strip	4	1″ x 1½″ x 13″	walnut
side trim	4	⅜″ x 1³⁄₁₆ x 12¾″	maple
glue			

Note: The pieces are cut 13″ long to allow for waste from the saw kerf.

Checker / Chess Board Plans

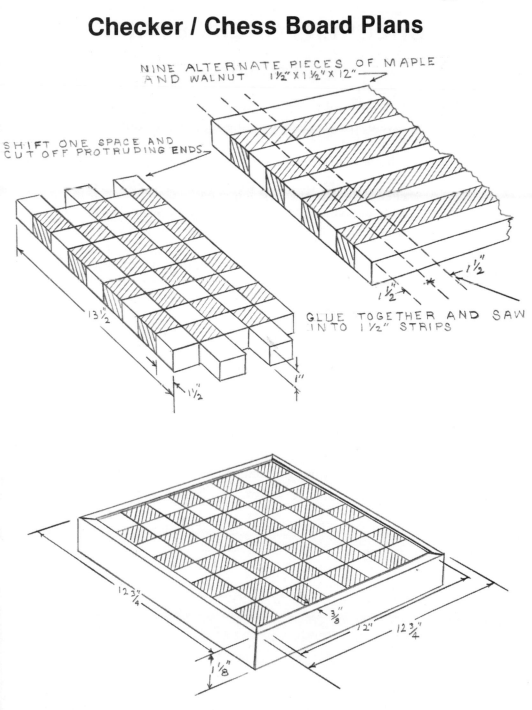

NINE ALTERNATE PIECES OF MAPLE AND WALNUT 1½" X 1½" X 12"

SHIFT ONE SPACE AND CUT OFF PROTRUDING ENDS

13½

1½

1"

GLUE TOGETHER AND SAW INTO 1½" STRIPS

1½

1½

12¾

3/8"

12"

12¾

1⅛"

CHECKER / CHESS BOARD

Procedure

1. Lay out and cut the nine 1 x 1½ x 13–inch strips. Five of the pieces should be maple and four should be walnut.
2. Glue and clamp the nine alternate strips together.
3. Clean and glue traces from the board, then proceed to plane the surface even.
4. Set the saw for a 1½–inch cut, then proceed to cut across the glued-up pieces. (Refer to drawing.)
5. Glue and clamp the eight 13½–inch pieces together. Be sure to shift one space for each piece. (Refer to drawing.)
6. Cut off the protruding ends to a 12–inch length. (Refer to drawing.)
7. Cut the trim pieces to the size indicated with 45–degree miter joints for the corners.
8. Glue and clamp the four pieces of trim to the board.
9. Sand the checker board to a smooth surface. Apply several coats of clear lacquer or polyurethane finish to the project, rub lightly between coats with fine steel wool or pumice and oil. Protect the finish by applying a coat of paste wax and buffing.

SPICE CABINET

10

Materials Required

Part	Number	Size	Material
back	1	½ " x 8½ " x 16"	pine or the wood of your choice
side	2	½ " x 4½ " x 13½ "	
base	1	½ " x 5½ " x 10"	
top shelf	1	½ " x 4½ " x 8½ "	
drawer divider	1	½ " x 4½ " x 10⅛ "	
drawer divider	4	½ " x 4½ " x 4 "	

Drawer parts:

front	1	½ " x 3¼ " x 3⅞ "	
side	2	¼ " x 3 " x 4½ "	
back	1	¼ " x 2¾ " x 3½ "	
bottom	1	¼ " x 3 " x 4½ "	
brads		¾ " finishing	
knob		½ "	
glue			

Spice Cabinet Plans

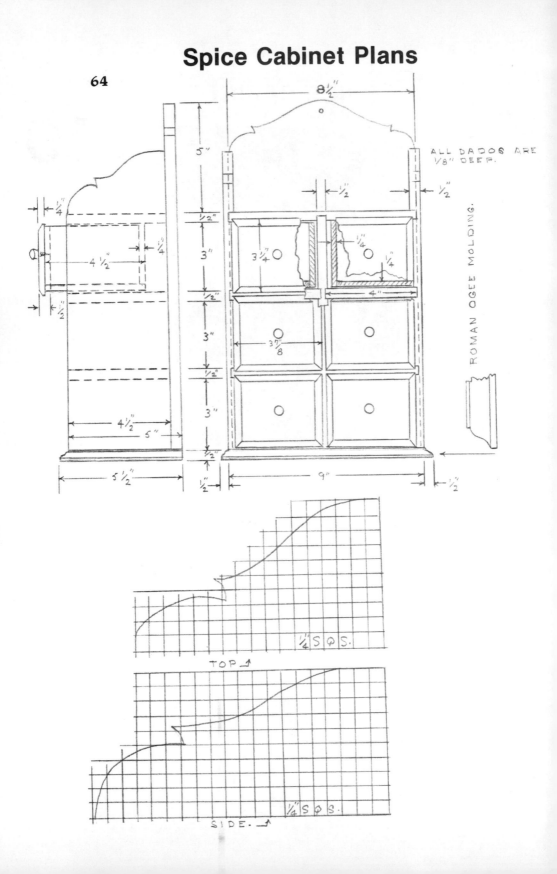

ALL DADOS ARE 1/8" DEEP.

ROMAN OGEE MOLDING.

1/4" SQS.

TOP

1/4" SQS.

SIDE.

Procedure

1. Lay out and cut the stock to the suggested size and shape.
2. Lay out and cut the matching dado joints into the sides and middle pieces. Cut a dado joint to the exact center of the top shelf.
3. Use a roman agee bit in a router or shaper to cut the design around the base.
4. Fasten the side pieces to the back, then attach the base. Continue to complete the assembly by fastening the pre-cut shelves into the dado joints. Glue and clamp to assembled the pieces.
5. Lay out and cut a ⅜–inch chamfer on the front piece of all six drawers, then continue to construct the small drawers. The front piece should have a ⅜ x ⅜–inch rabbet joint cut on the two sides and bottom to receive the ¼–inch plywood sides and bottom. The drawer units should be assembled with glue and ¾–inch finishing brads.
6. Clean all traces of glue, set and fill all nail holes, and proceed to sand the project to a smooth surface.
7. Select and apply the colored stain or paint of your choice. When dry, apply several coats of clear oil finish; rub lightly between coats with fine steel wool or pumice and oil. Protect the finish with paste wax.
8. Install your choice of ½–inch knob on each drawer front.

NAPKIN HOLDER I

11

Materials Required

Part	Number	Size	Material
base	1	½ " x 7¼ " x 8¾ "	cherry or the wood of your choice
hold down			
bar	1	½ " x 1¼ " x 8¾ "	
dowel	3	1½ " dia. x 5"	
glue			

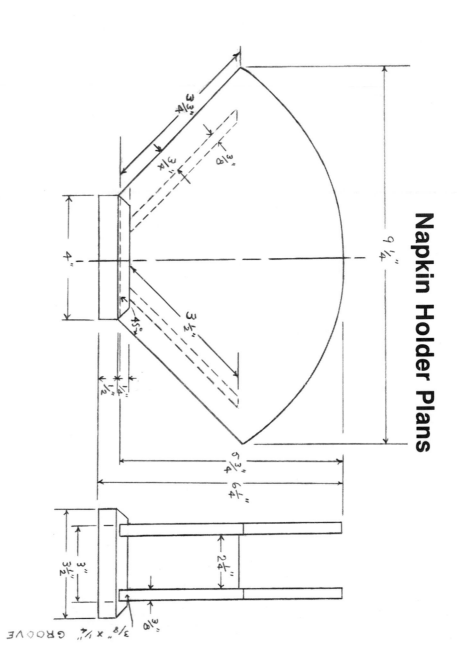

Napkin Holder Plans

3¾"

¾"

3⁄8"

4"

45°

3½"

1½"

1¼"

9¼"

5¾"

6¼"

3"

3½"

2¼"

3⁄8"

3/8" x ¼" GROOVE

NAPKIN HOLDER I

Procedure

1. Lay out and cut all pieces to the suggested size.
2. Locate and bore two ½–inch diameter holes through the base, then lay out and bore two $\frac{9}{16}$–inch diameter holes through the hold down bar.
3. With a router and cove bit cut the design on the base. A chamfered cut is equally attractive.
4. Insert the two ½–inch diameter dowels into the holes with glue.
5. Scrape all traces of glue, then sand the napkin holder to a smooth surface.
6. Select and apply the stain or paint of your choice. When dry, apply several coats of clear finishing oil, rubbing between coats with fine steel wool or pumice and lemon oil. Protect the finish by applying a coat of paste wax and buffing.

NAPKIN HOLDER II

12

Materials Required

Part	Number	Size	Material
fan shaped side	2	⅜″ x 5¾″ x 9¼″	maple or the wood of your choice
side	2	⅜″ x 2¼″ x 3½″	walnut or the wood of your choice
base	1	¾″ x 3½″ x 4″	walnut or the wood of your choice
glue			

Napkin Holder Plans

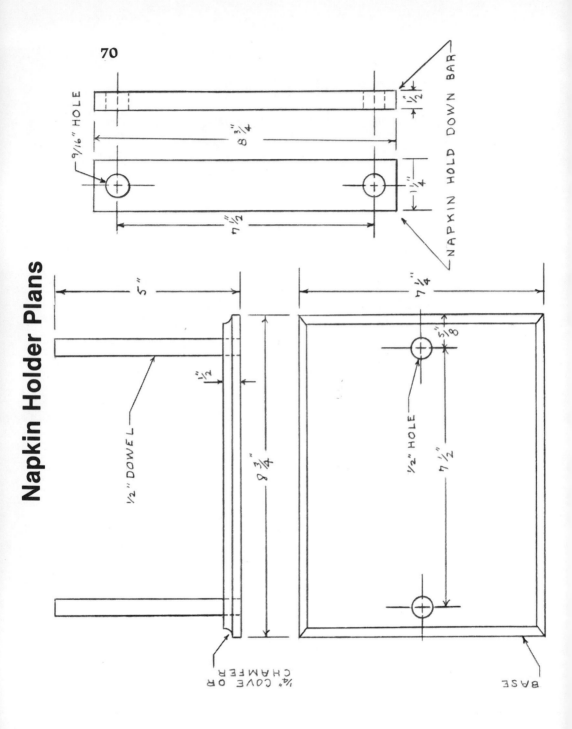

9/16" HOLE

8 3/4

7 1/2

1 1/4

1/2

NAPKIN HOLD DOWN BAR

5"

1/2" DOWEL

1/2

8 3/4

1/8" COVE OR CHAMFER

7 1/4

5/8"

1/2" HOLE

7 1/2

BASE

Procedure

1. Lay out and cut the base to the size indicated on the drawing.
2. Lay out and cut the two ⅜ x ¼–inch grooves into the base.
3. Lay out and cut the ⅜–inch chamfered design on the base.
4. Fasten the two fan–shaped sides into the grooves with glue, then fasten the two end pieces to the fan–shaped sides by gluing and clamping.
5. Scrape all traces of glue, set and fill all nail holes, then sand the napkin holder to a smooth surface.
6. Select and apply the stain or paint of your choice. When dry, apply several coats of clear lacquer finish, rubbing between coats with fine steel wool or pumice and lemon oil. Protect the finish by applying a coat of paste wax and buffing.

COLONIAL MIRROR

13

Materials Required

Part	Number	Size	Material
top of frame	1	¾ " x 6" x 19"	pine or the wood of your choice
bottom of frame	1	¾ " x 4" x 19"	
side	2	¾ " x 3" x 21"	
mirror	1	⅛ " x 14" x 16"	to be purchased at a local glass dealer
dowels (optional)	8	⅜ " x ¾"	

Colonial Mirror Plans

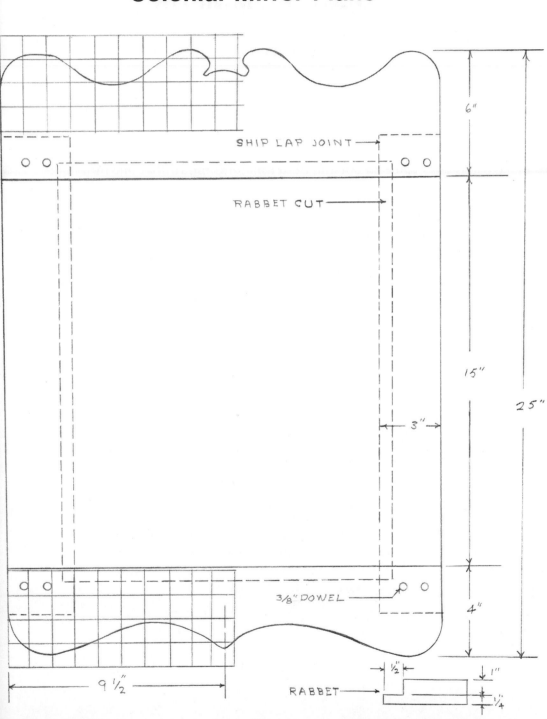

SHIP LAP JOINT

RABBET CUT

6"

15"

25"

3"

3/8" DOWEL

4"

9 1/2"

RABBET

1/2"

1"

1/4"

COLONIAL MIRROR

Procedure

1. Cut the stock to the dimensions given. Do not cut out the design until the joints are cut.
2. Lay out and cut the ship lap recess into the top and bottom pieces of the frame. The recess should be half the thickness of the stock (⅜ inch). Continue to cut the matching end lap rabbet cut into the sides of the frame. Again the cut should be half the thickness of the wood (⅜ inch).
3. Lay out and cut the design on the top and bottom pieces of the frame.
4. Lay out and cut a ¼ x ½–inch rabbet cut on the back inside edge of all four pieces. This recess will receive the mirror when the frame is constructed.
5. Fasten the four pieces to the frame into the pre-cut ship lap joint using glue and clamps. If dowel pins are to be used in the frame for support, allow the glue to dry, then bore the four holes completely through the correct location. Insert the dowel pins with glue.
6. Clean all traces of glue and continue to sand the mirror frame to smooth surface.
7. Select and apply the colored stain or paint of your choice. When dry, apply several coats of clear polyurethane finish. Rub between each coat with fine steel wool or pumice and oil. Protect the finish with paste wax.
8. Install the mirror into the recessed rabbet joint on the back of the frame by using glass points or thin wood strips screwed into the back of the frame and over the edge of the mirror.

MAIL BOX

14

Materials Required

Part	Number	Size	Material
back	1	½ " x 9½ " x 14"	mahogany or the wood of your choice
side	2	½ " x 5¾ " x 6½ "	
top	1	½ " x 1" x 14"	
lid	1	½ " x 6" x 14"	
bottom	1	½ " x 4¾ " x 13"	
Butt hinges	2	1"	
glue			
nails		#4 finishing	

Mail Box Plans

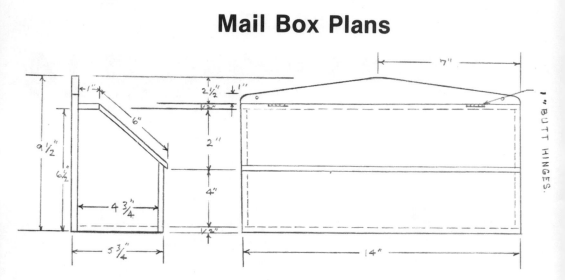

Procedure

1. Lay out and cut all parts to the suggested size and design.
2. Fasten the sides to the back, then fasten the bottom to the back and side pieces. Cut the top edge of the front piece to a 40–degree angle, then fasten the front to the sides and bottom. Use glue and #4 finishing nails.
3. Lay out and cut the top and bottom edge of the lid to a 40–degree angle.
4. Lay out and cut the four $\frac{1}{16}$ x 1–inch gains to receive the two butt hinges. Attach the two 1–inch butt hinges to the top piece and to the lid, then continue to fasten the top piece to the top of the sides with glue and 4 finishing nails.
5. Clean all traces of glue, set and fill all nail holes, and continue to sand the box to a smooth surface.
6. Select and apply the colored paint or stain of your choice. When dry, apply several coats of spar varnish, rubbing between coats with fine steel wool or pumice and oil. To protect the finish use paste wax and buff.

Note: Spar varnish is the best available finish for outdoor use, as it repels moisture and salt.

CANDLE STAND

15

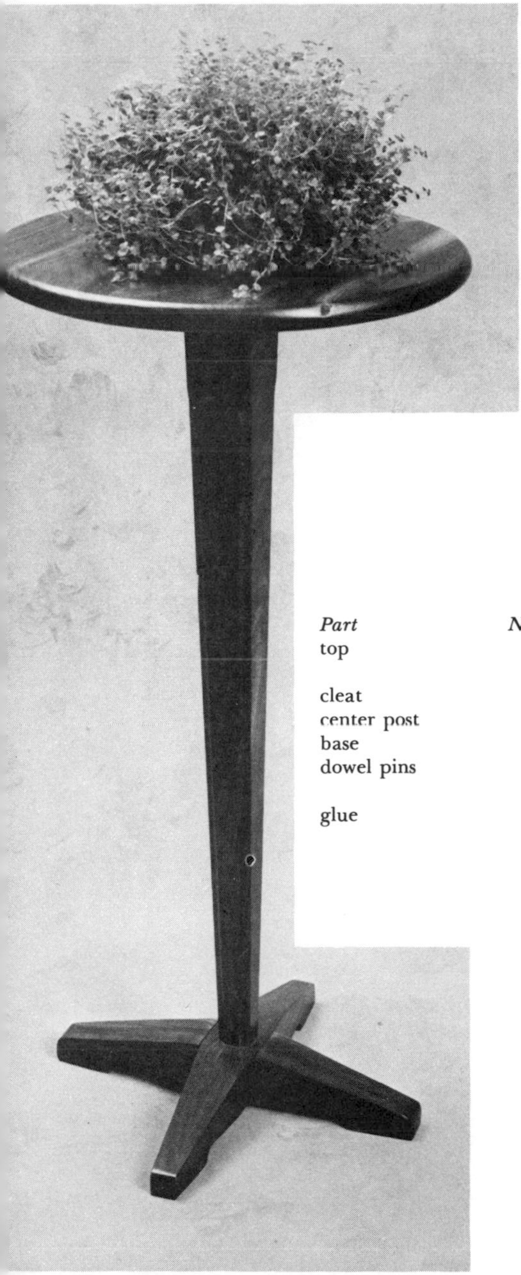

Materials Required

Part	*Number*	*Size*	*Material*
top	1	¾″ x 13″ x 13″	walnut or the wood of your choice
cleat	1	¾″ x 2″ x 10″	
center post	1	2¼″ x 2¼″ x 22″	
base	2	2″ x 2″ x 12″	
dowel pins	2	½″ x 2¾″ ½″ x ¾″	birch
glue			

Candle Stand Plans

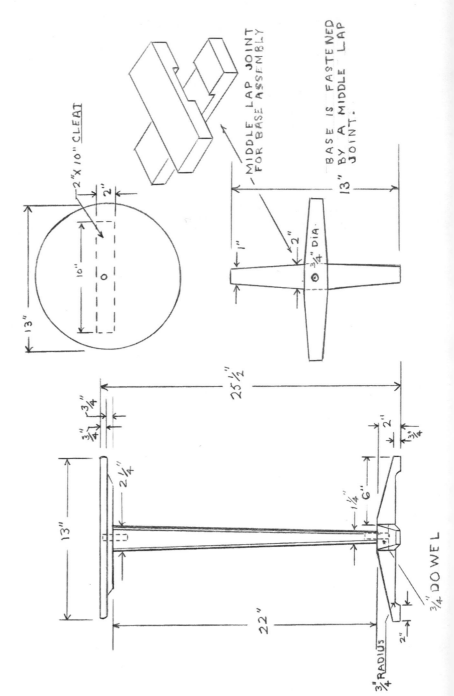

2"X 10" CLEAT

2"

13"

16"

MIDDLE LAP JOINT
FOR BASE ASSEMBLY

BASE IS FASTENED
BY A MIDDLE LAP
JOINT.

13"

1"

2"

3/4" DIA.

3/4"
3/4"
3"

25 1/2"

13"

2 1/4"

22"

1 1/4"

6"

2"

3/4"

3/4" DOWEL

3/4" RADIUS

2"

Procedure

1. Glue and clamp up the stock to the size indicated. Lay out and cut the top piece to the suggested design.
2. Cut a 45–degree bevel on both ends of the 2 x 10–inch cleat, then fasten the cleat beneath the top by gluing and clamping.
3. Locate the center on both ends of the center post, then bore a ½–inch diameter hole to a depth of 1½ inches into both ends.
4. Lay out and cut the taper on the center post. After planing the four sides even, lay out and cut the ⅜–inch chamfer on the four edges of the center post.
5. Before cutting the design on the two base pieces, lay out and cut the middle half lap joint, then proceed to lay out and cut the design on the two base pieces. Fasten the two base pieces to the middle half lap joint by gluing and clamping.
6. Bore a ½–inch hole to a depth of 1¼ inches through the cleat and top. Bore a ½–inch hole to a depth of 1¾ inches through the center of the base.
7. Assemble all of the pieces together with ½–inch diameter dowels pins glued into the pre-bored holes.
8. Scrape all traces of glue, then sand the stand to a smooth surface.
9. Select and apply the stain or paint of your choice. When dry, apply several coats of finishing oil, rubbing between coats with fine steel wool or pumice and oil. Protect the finish with a coat of paste wax, and then buff.

JEWEL BOX

16

Materials Required

Part	Number	Size	Material
base	1	⅜″ x 4½″ x 9¼″	walnut
top	1	½″ x 4½″ x 9¼″	walnut
side	2	½″ x 3⅛″ x 9½″	maple
side	2	½″ x 3⅛″ x 4¾″	maple
knobs	1	½″ diameter	porcelain or brass
brads		1″ finishing	

Jewel Box Plans

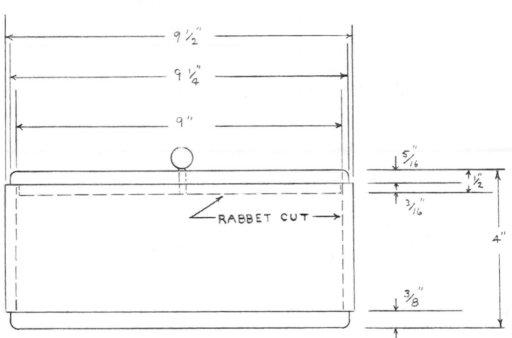

9 1/2"

9 1/4"

9 "

RABBET CUT

5/16"

1/2"

3/16"

4"

3/8"

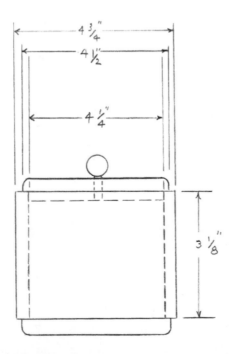

4 3/4"

4 1/2"

4 1/4"

3 1/8"

JEWEL BOX

Procedure

1. Lay out and cut all pieces to the suggested size.
2. Lay out and cut the two $\frac{1}{4}$" x $\frac{1}{2}$" rabbet joints on the front and back pieces. Lay out and cut the $\frac{3}{16}$" x $\frac{1}{4}$" rabbet cut completely around the bottom edge of the lid. This cut will allow the top lid to fit snugly into the box.
3. Fasten the sides together using glue and 1" finishing brads. Fasten the base to the box using glue and 1" finishing brads.
4. Locate the center of the top lid and drill an $\frac{1}{8}$" hole to receive the stem for the $\frac{1}{2}$" knob.
5. Scrape all traces of glue, set and fill all holes then sand the box to a smooth surface.
6. Apply several coats of clear lacquer finish rubbing between coats with fine steel wool or pumice and oil. Protect the finish with a coat of paste wax and buff.
7. Attach a porcelain or brass knob to the $\frac{1}{8}$" pre-drilled hole in the top.

DESK LIGHTERS

17

Materials Required

Part	Number	Size	Material
Square lighter:			
block	1	2" x 2" x 2"	cherry or the wood of your choice
lighter cylinder	1	1¼" dia.	
Octagon lighter:			
block	1	2¼" x 4" x 4"	walnut or the wood of your choice
lighter cylinder	1	1¼" dia.	

Note: The lighter cylinder and well can be purchased at a local craft supply store.

Desk Lighters Plans

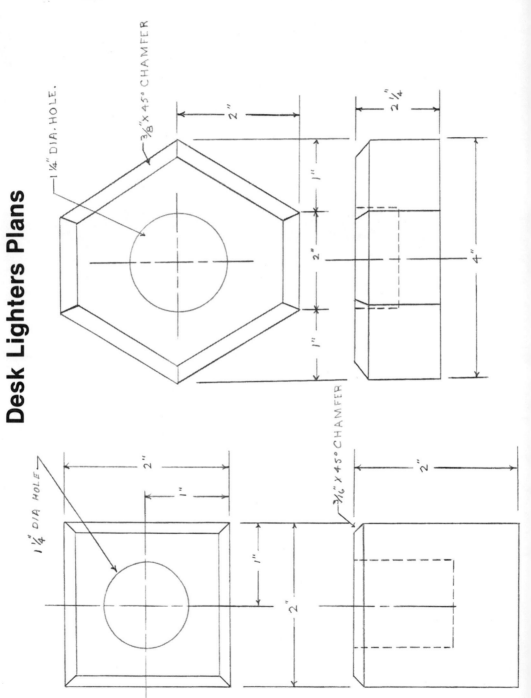

DESK LIGHTERS

Procedure

1. Lay out and cut the lighter block to the size indicated on the drawing.
2. Lay out and cut the chamfered design to the size indicated on the drawing.
3. Locate and mark the center of the block, then proceed to bore a 1¼–inch diameter hole. The depth of the hole is determined by the lighter cylinder well.
4. Sand the lighter block to a smooth surface, then apply several coats of finishing oil. Rub between each coat with fine steel wool or pumice and oil. Protect the finish with a coat of paste wax.
5. Insert the lighter well into the 1¼–inch hole; then place the lighter cylinder into the well.

Note: The lighters may be purchased in various sizes and shapes.

BLACKBOARD PHONE SHELF

Materials Required

Part	Number	Size	Material
blackboard back	1	¼" x 15½" x 26"	hardboard painted with blackboard paint
side	2	⅝" x 10½" x 27"	pine or the material of your choice
bottom shelf	1	⅝" x 10½" x 15½"	
middle shelf	1	⅝" x 10½" x 15½"	
top shelf	1	⅝" x 2½" x 15½"	
top decorative piece	1	⅝" x 2½" x 15"	
bottom back piece	1	⅝" x 1⅝" x 15"	
key rack	1	⅝" x 1⅝" x 15"	
glue			
brads			
cuphooks	6	¾" finishing ¾" diameter	
blackboard paint			

Blackboard Phone Shelf Plans

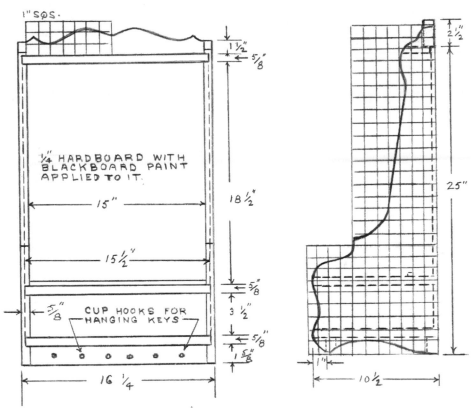

1" SQS.

¼ HARDBOARD WITH BLACKBOARD PAINT APPLIED TO IT.

CUP HOOKS FOR HANGING KEYS

15"

15½"

16¼

1½"

5/8

18½"

5/8

3½"

5/8

1 5/8"

2½"

25"

1"

10½

Procedure

1. Lay out and cut all pieces to the suggested size and design.
2. Lay out and cut the three ¼ x ⅝-inch dado joints.
3. Lay out and cut the ¼ x ⅜-inch rabbet joint on the back edge of both side pieces. The rabbet cut is made to recess the black–board.
4. Fasten the three shelves to the dado joints in the side pieces by gluing and clamping.
5. Make the 15½ x 26-inch blackboard by cutting a piece of hardboard, then applying two coats of

BLACKBOARD PHONE SHELF

special blackboard paint to the smooth side of the hardboard. The paint can be purchased at your local paintstore.

6. Fasten the blackboard to the back by gluing and nailing into the rabbet joints.

7. Attach the top decorative piece to the top shelf by gluing and clamping. Locate and fasten the cup hooks to the $1\frac{5}{8}$–inch stock, then glue the key rack to the bottom shelf.

8. Scrape all traces of glue, set and fill all nail holes, then proceed to sand your project to a smooth surface.

9. Select and apply the colored stain or paint of your choice. When dry, apply several coats of lacquer. Rub between coats with fine steel wool or pumice and oil. Protect the finish by applying a coat of paste wax and buffing.

CANDLE SCONCE

19

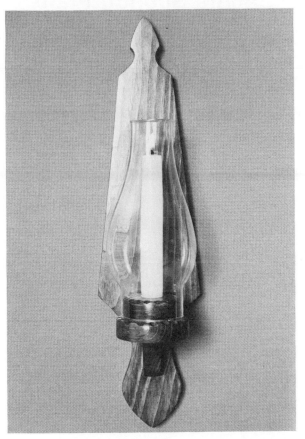

Materials Required

Part	Number	Size	Material
back	1	¾″ x 5″ x 18″	pine or the wood of your choice
bracket	1	¾″ x 2½″ x 3¾″	
disk	1	¾″ x 2¾″ dia.	
disk	1	¾″ x 2⅜ dia.	

Note 1: A metal inset or candle cup can be purchased at your local craft supply store.

Note 2: The disks are made to hold a 2½″ diameter glass chimney. The glass chimney can be purchased at your local hardware or craft supply store.

Candle Sconce Plans

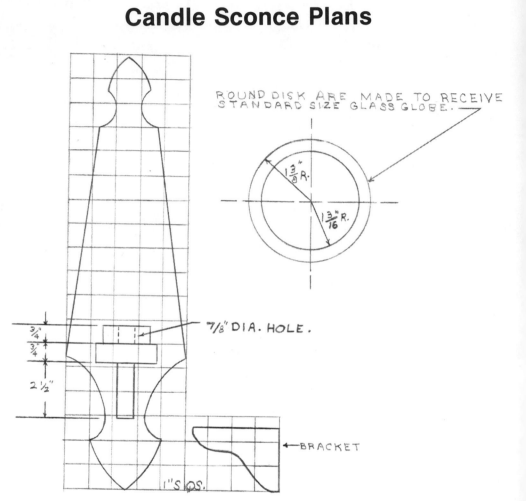

ROUND DISK ARE MADE TO RECEIVE
STANDARD SIZE GLASS GLOBE.

$1\frac{3}{8}$" R.

$1\frac{3}{16}$" R.

$\frac{3}{4}$"

$\frac{3}{4}$"

$2\frac{1}{2}$"

$\frac{7}{8}$" DIA. HOLE.

←BRACKET

1" SQS.

Procedure

1. Lay out and cut all of the pieces to the suggested size and design.
2. If a candle cup is not used, bore a ⅞–inch hole through the center of the 2⅜–inch diameter disk to hold the candle. A ⅞–inch diameter metal inset can be inserted into the hole. If a candle cup is used, glue and clamp it to the top disk.

CANDLE SCONCE

3. Glue and clamp the small disk to the large disk, making sure the small disk is centered over the larger one.
4. Assemble the two disks to the bracket by gluing and clamping.
5. Fasten the bracket and disk assembly to the back by drilling a countersunk pilot hole through the back and into the bracket, then attach with two #8, 1½–inch flathead wood screws.
6. Scrape all traces of glue, then sand the sconce to a smooth surface.
7. Select and apply the stain of your choice. When dry, apply several coats of clear finishing oil, rubbing between each coat with fine steel wool or pumice or oil. Protect the finish with a coat of paste wax and buff.

PLANT STAND

20

Materials Required

Part	Number	Size	Material
base	1	¾ " x 14 " dia.	pine or the wood of your choice
base	4	½ " x 3 " dia.	
plate	4	½ " x 2½ " dia.	
top	4	½ " x 6 " dia.	
dowel	4	½ " x 12 "	birch
		½ " x 18 "	
		½ " x 24 "	
		½ " x 30 "	
glue			

Plant Stand Plans

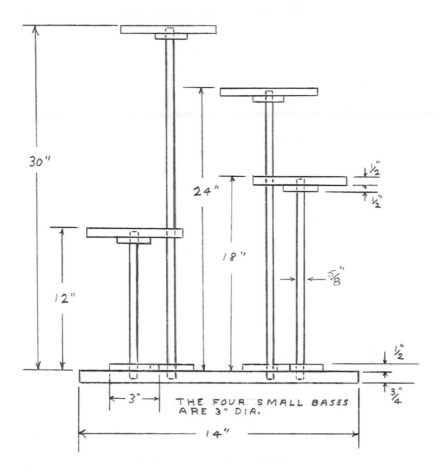

30"

24"

18"

12"

½"

½"

⅝"

½"

¾"

←3"→

THE FOUR SMALL BASES
ARE 3" DIA.

14"

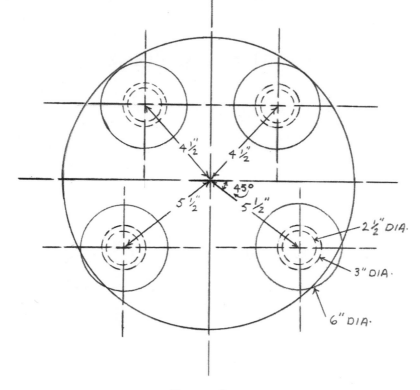

Procedure

1. Lay out and cut all of the pieces to the suggested diameters.
2. Locate and fasten the four ½ x 2½–inch diameter plates beneath the four stand tops.
3. Locate and fasten the four ½ x 3–inch diameter bases to the large 14–inch diameter base.
4. Lay out and bore a ½–inch hole to a depth of ¾ of an inch through the center of the four 2½–inch diameter underplates and the four 3–inch diameter bases.
5. Before attaching the ½–inch dowels, sand all of the pieces to a smooth surface.
6. Insert glue into the pre-bored holes, then assemble the dowel to the plates and base.
7. Select and apply the stain or paint of your choice. When dry, apply several coats of clear polyurethane or lacquer finish, rubbing between each coat with fine steel wool or pumice and oil. Protect the finish with a coat of paste wax, and then buff.

SPICE RACK

Materials Required

Part	Number	Size	Material
back	1	½ " x 11" x 19½ "	cherry or the wood of your choice
side	2	½ " x 2" x 3¼ "	
shelf	2	⅜ " x 2" x 3¼ "	
bars	4	¼ " x ¾ " x 11"	maple
brads		1" finishing	
wood screws	8	#6 1 " flathead	
glue			

96

Spice Rack Plans

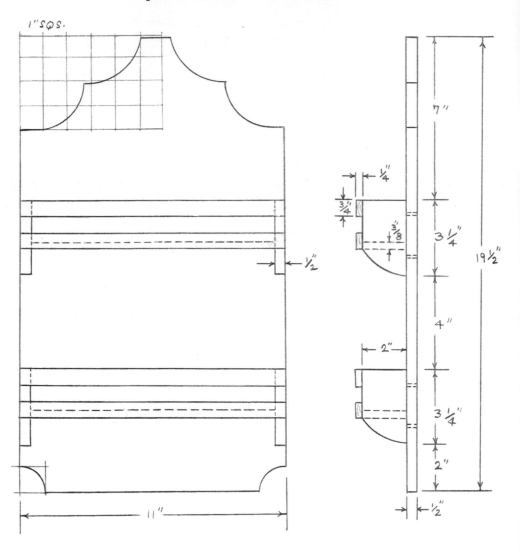

SPICE RACK

Procedure

1. Glue up and clamp the stock to the required width. Lay out and cut all pieces to the suggested size and design.
2. Attach the shelves to the side pieces, then fasten the ¾ x 11–inch bars to the front of the assembly, using glue and 1–inch finishing brads.
3. Locate and drill two countersunk pilot holes through the back and into each side piece, then proceed to fasten the shelf assembly to the back with #6, 1–inch flathead wood screws.
4. Scrape all traces of glue, set and fill all nail holes, then file and sand the spice rack to a smooth surface.
5. Select and apply the stain or paint of your choice. When dry, apply several coats of clear polyurethane finish, rubbing between coats with fine steel wool or pumice and oil. Protect the finish by applying a coat of paste wax and buffing.

CRIBBAGE BOARD

22

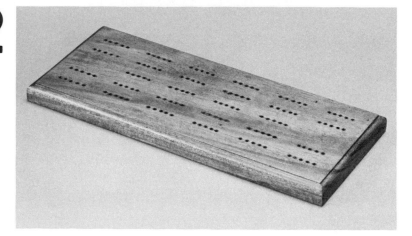

Materials Required

Part	Number	Size	Material
board	1	¾ " x 6" x 14¼ "	cherry or the wood of your choice
dowels (for pegs)		⅛" x 36"	

Procedure

1. Lay out and cut the board to the size indicated.
2. Lay out the ⅛–inch diameter peg holes according to the dimensions on the drawing.
3. Drill the 140 peg holes to a depth of ½ inch. Be careful in aligning the holes.
4. Cut a ⅛–inch diameter dowel to a length of 1 inch to make the pegs.
5. With a router and quarter round bit, cut the design on the board. A chamfer is equally attractive.
6. Sand the board to a smooth surface.
7. Select and apply the stain or paint of your choice. When dry, apply several coats of lacquer, rubbing between coats with fine steel wool or pumice and lemon oil. Protect the finish by applying a coat of paste wax and buffing.

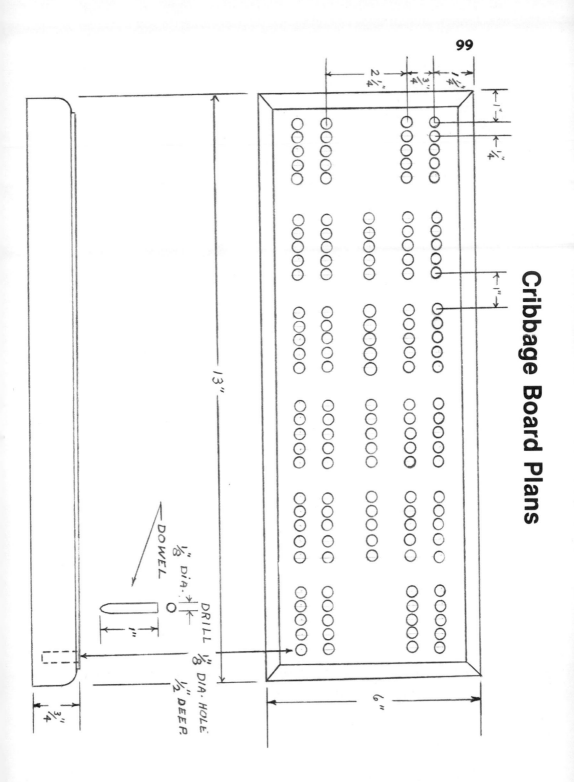

Cribbage Board Plans

FOOT STOOL

23

Materials Required

Part	Number	Size	Material
top	1	¾ " x 6½ " x 13 "	maple or the wood of your choice
brace	2	¾ " x 1¾ " x 11 "	
legs	2	¾ " x 7" x 7"	
dowel plugs	8	³⁄₈ " x ³⁄₈ "	
glue			
wood screws	8	#9 1½ " flathead	

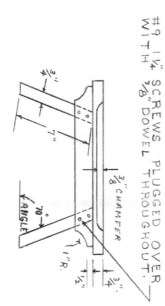

#9 1¼" SCREWS PLUGGED OVER
WITH ⅜" DOWEL THROUGHOUT.

⅜" CHAMFER

70° ANGLE

1" R.

⅜"

½"

¾"

7"

¾"

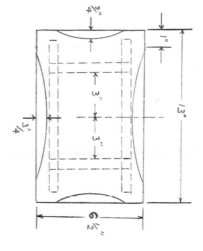

¾"

1"

13"

¾"

3"

3"

6½"

¾"

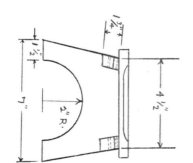

1½"

1¾"

4"

2" R.

4½"

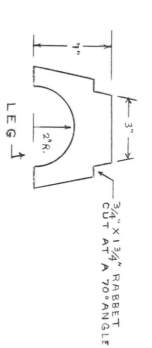

LEG

4"

3"

2" R.

¾" X 1¾" RABBET
CUT AT A 70° ANGLE

Foot Stool Plans

FOOT STOOL

Procedure

1. Lay out and cut the top to the size indicated, then lay out and cut the ¾–inch chamfer around the top.
2. Lay out and cut the two legs to the suggested size and design. Make sure the 70–degree angle is cut on the top and bottom. Lay out and cut two ¾ x 1¾–inch rabbet joints on each leg. Make sure to cut the rabbets at a 70–degree angle.
3. Lay out and cut the two side braces, then locate and drill four counterbored pilot holes through each brace. Fasten the braces to the legs with #9, 1½–inch plathead wood screws. Plug the ⅜–inch counterbored holes with ⅜–inch birch dowel plugs.
4. Attach the leg and brace assembly to the top by gluing and clamping.
5. Scrape all traces of glue then sand the stool to a smooth surface.
6. Select and apply the stain or paint of your choice. When dry, apply several coats of clear polyurethane finish, rubbing between each coat with fine steel or pumice or oil. Protect the finish by applying a coat of paste wax and buffing.

WALL BOX

Materials Required

Part	Number	Size	Material
back	1	⅜″ x 9½″ x 17″	pine or material of your choice
sides	2	⅜″ x 6½″ x 11″	
lid	1	⅜″ x 7½″ x 11½″	
shelf & bottom	2	⅜″ x 6″ x 9½″	
front	1	⅜″ x 8¼″ x 10½″	
drawer, side	2	⅜″ x 1½″ x 5½″	
drawer, front & back	2	⅜″ x 1½″ x 8¼″	
drawer bottom	1	¼″ x 5½″ x 8¼″	
false drawer front	1	⅜″ x 2″ x 8¾″	
brads		1″	
butt hinges	2	1″	
glue			

Wall Box Plans

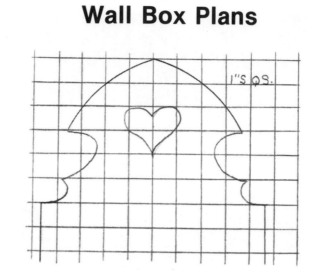

1"SQS.

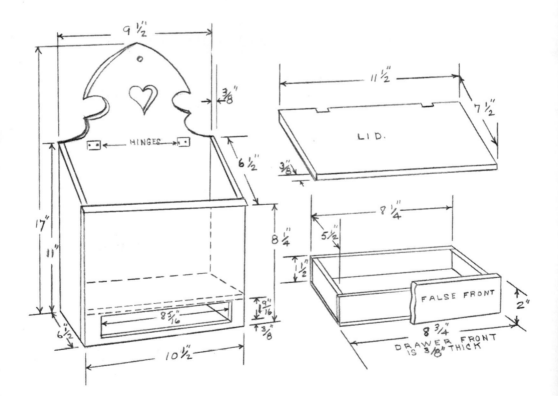

9 1/2"

3/8"

HINGES

6 1/2"

17"

11"

8 1/4"

9/16"

3/8"

8 5/16"

6 1/2"

10 1/2"

11 1/2"

7 1/2"

LID.

3/8"

8 1/4"

5 1/2"

1 1/2"

FALSE FRONT

2"

8 3/4"

DRAWER FRONT
IS 3/8" THICK

WALL BOX

Procedure

1. Lay out and cut the stock to the suggested size and design.
2. Fasten the two sides to the back using glue and 1–inch finishing brads.
3. Fasten the shelf and bottom to the sides using glue and 1–inch brads.
4. The top edge of the front piece should be cut at a 30–degree angle to match the angle of the side pieces. Pre–cut the opening for the drawer in the front piece and continue to fasten the front to the sides using glue and 1–inch brads.
5. Cut the front and back edge of the lid to a 30–degree angle. Chisel cut the two ⅛ x 1–inch gains on the back edge of the lid to receive the 1–inch butt hinges. Proceed to attach the hinges to the lid and the back of the box.
6. Construct the drawer by fastening a simple box together and attaching the false front to the box using glue and 1–inch brads.
7. Attach a small pull knob of your choice to the center of the drawer front.
8. Set and fill all holes and continue to sand the wall box to a smooth finished surface.
9. Select and apply the stain or paint of your choice. When the project has dried, apply several coats of finishing oil or polyurethane. Rub between each coat with fine steel wool or pumice and oil. Protect the finish with paste wax.

CANDLESTICKS

25

Materials Required

Part	Number	Size	Material
large candlestick	1	2¼″ x 2¼″ x 13″	walnut or the wood of your choice
mid-size candlestick	1	2″ x 2″ x 12″	
small candlestick	1	1¾″ x 1¾″ x 11″	
brass candle inset	3	¾″ dia.	

Note: Although the brass candle insets add to the design of the candlesticks, they are not necessary. Insets can be purchased from your local craft supply store.

Candlesticks Plans

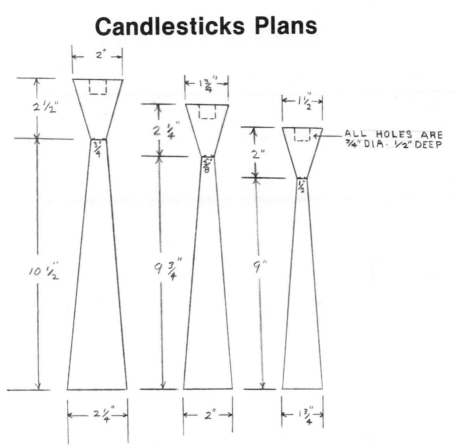

Procedure

1. Glue up and clamp the three pieces to the suggested thickness.
2. Lay out and cut the three pieces to the suggested size and design. The design is the same on all sides.
3. On the top of each candlestick locate the center then bore a ⅞–inch diameter hole to a depth of ½ inch. Insert a ⅞–inch diameter brass candle inset into each hole.
4. Sand the candlesticks to a smooth surface.
5. Apply several coats of clear finishing oil, rubbing between coats with fine steel wool or pumice and lemon oil. Protect the finish by applying a coat of paste wax and buffing.

KITCHEN UTENSIL RACK

Materials Required

Part	Number	Size	Material
back	1	½ " x 14¼ " x 14¾ "	birch, maple, or pine
strip dividing	2	⅜ " x ⅞ " x 13¼ "	walnut or cherry
blocks	2	¼ " x ¾ " x ⅞ "	walnut or cherry
wood screws		#5 ¾ " flathead	

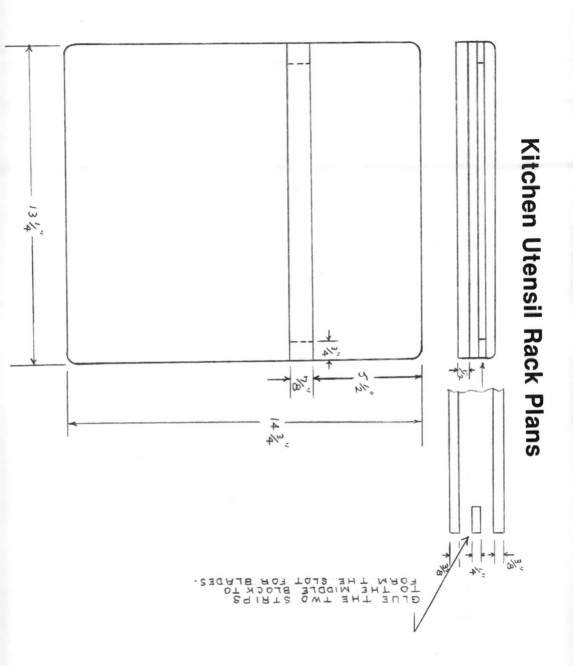

Kitchen Utensil Rack Plans

13½"

14¾"

5½"

⅛"

¾"

½"

⅜"

¼"

⅜"

GLUE THE TWO STRIPS
TO THE MIDDLE BLOCK TO
FORM THE SLOT FOR BLADES.

KITCHEN UTENSIL RACK

Procedure

1. Lay out and cut all pieces to the suggested size and design.
2. Glue and clamp the two ⅜ x 13¼–inch strips to the two ¼ x ⅞–inch pieces.
3. Attach the utensil holder to the back piece by gluing and clamping. When the glue dries, reinforce the holder by drilling two countersunk pilot holes through the back and into the holder. Screw in two #5, ¾–inch flathead wood screws.
4. To hang the rack drill two ⅜–inch holes to a depth of ⅝ inches. The holes should be aligned and 11 inches apart through the back of the rack.
5. Clean all traces of glue, then sand the utensil rack to a smooth finish.
6. Select and apply the stain or paint of your choice. When dry, apply several coats of clear finishing oil. Rub between coats with fine steel wool or pumice and oil. Rub between coats with fine steel wool or pumice and oil. Protect the surface with a coat of paste wax and buff.

PIPE BOX

Materials Required

Part	Number	Size	Material
back	1	³⁄₈″ x 5″ x 16½″	pine or the wood of your choice
side	2	³⁄₈″ x 3″ x 11″	
front	1	³⁄₈″ x 5″ x 5¾″	
shelf	1	³⁄₈″ x 3″ x 4¼″	
base	1	½″ x 4″ x 5½″	
drawer parts			
false front	1	³⁄₈″ x 3″ x 5″	
front, back	2	³⁄₈″ x 3″ x 3³⁄₈″	
side	2	³⁄₈″ x 3″ x 2¾″	
bottom	1	³⁄₈″ x 2″ x 3³⁄₈″	
knob		1″ dia.	brass or wood
glue			

Pipe Box Plans

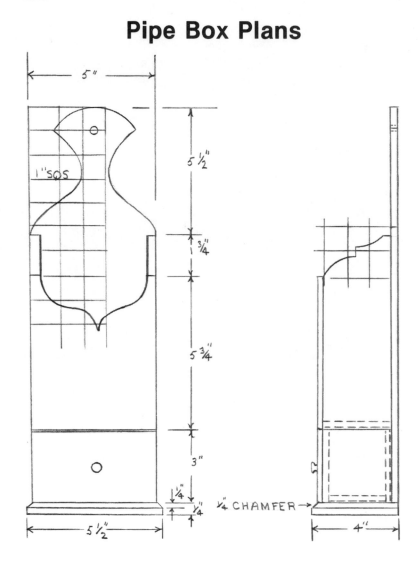

5"

5 ½"

¾"

5 ¾"

3"

¼"

¼"

1"SQS

5 ½"

¼ CHAMFER→

4"

GLUE FRONT TO DRAWER BOX

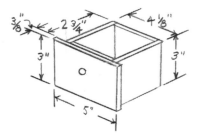

⅜"

2 ¾"

4 ⅛"

3"

3"

5"

PIPE BOX

Procedure

1. Lay out and cut all pieces to the suggested size and design.
2. Fasten the sides to the back, then fasten the shelf to the sides. Continue to attach the front to the sides, using glue and 1–inch finishing brads.
3. Lay out and cut a ¼–inch chamfer on the base, then attach the base to the box assembly with glue and 1–inch finishing brads.
4. Construct the small drawer to the dimensions given in the drawing. The false front is attached to the drawer by gluing and clamping.
5. Locate the center of the drawer and drill a ⅛–inch diameter hole to fasten the ½–inch diameter brass knob.
6. Scrape all traces of glue, set and fill all nail holes, then sand the pipe box to a smooth surface.
7. Select and apply the stain or paint of your choice. When dry, apply several coats of clear polyurethane finish, rubbing between coats with fine steel wool or pumice and oil. Protect the finish by applying a coat of paste wax and buffing.

KNIFE HOLDER

Materials Required

Part	Number	Size	Materials
base	1	½ " x 3 " x 7¾ "	cherry or the wood of your choice
front section	1	2 " x 6¾ " x 8½ "	
back section	1	½ " x 6¾ " x 8½ "	
screws	4	#10, 1¼ " flathead	

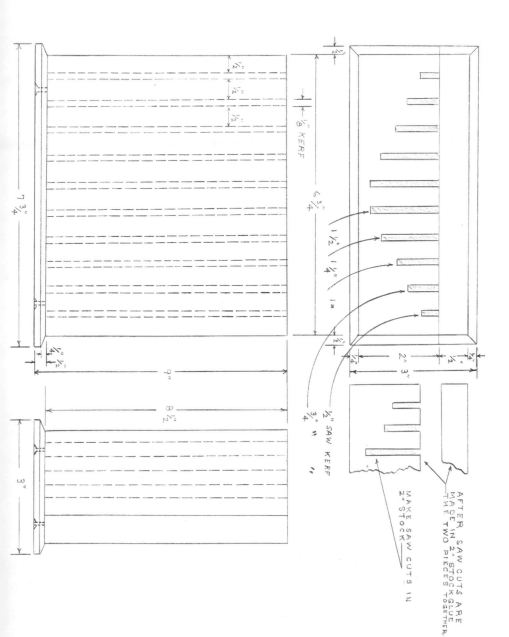

Knife Holder Plans

KNIFE HOLDER

Procedure

1. Lay out and cut the three pieces to the suggested size. You may have to glue up stock to achieve the correct thickness.
2. Lay out the exact location for the knife slots. Proceed to cut the slots on the back side of the front piece, making sure that the saw blade cut is to the correct depth for each knife slot. Fasten the back piece to the front to enclose the knife slots. Use glue and clamps.
3. Lay out and cut a ¼ x ½–inch chamfer or cove design around the top edge of the base.
4. Fasten the base to the bottom of the knife block by drilling four pilot countersunk holes, then screwing four #10, 1¼–inch flathead screws.
5. Clean all traces of glue and proceed to sand the project to a smooth surface.
6. Apply several coats of clear finishing oil, rubbing between each coat with fine steel wool or pumice and oil. Protect the finish with paste wax.

MAGAZINE RACK

29

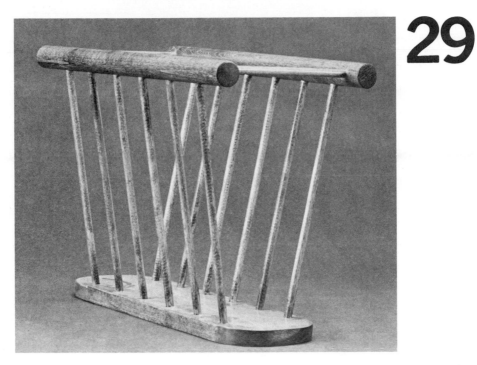

Materials Required

Part	Number	Size	Material
dowel	12	⅜″ x 12″	birch
dowel	2	⅜″ x 6″	birch
dowel	2	1½″ x 17½″	birch
base	1	¾″ x 5½″ x 17½″	birch

Magazine Rack Plans

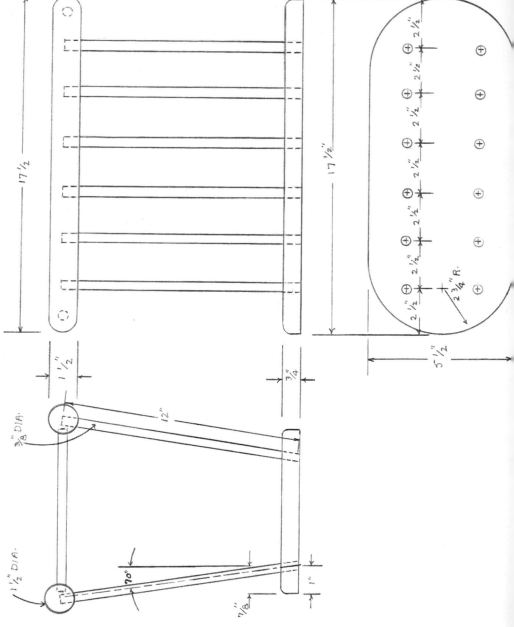

MAGAZINE RACK

Procedure

1. Lay out and cut all parts to the suggested size.
2. Lay out the location and bore all holes in the base. The twelve ⅜–inch diameter holes bored in the base should be positioned at a 70–degree angle. To assure the correct angles set a sliding T-bevel to 70 degrees to check the angle of the bit cut.
3. Lay out the location and drill all the ⅜–inch diameter holes ¾ of an inch into the two 1½–inch diameter dowels. Make sure all of the holes are bored at a 90–degree angle to the work and in a straight line. Locate and bore four ⅜–inch diameter holes to receive the two end dowels. The holes are bored to a ⅜–inch depth.
4. Fasten all of the pieces into the pre-drilled holes.
5. Clean all traces of glue and continue to sand the project to a smooth surface.
6. Select and apply the colored stain or paint of your choice. When dry, apply several coats of clear lacquer or polyurethane finish. Rub between each coat with fine steel wool or pumice and oil. Preserve the finish with lemon oil.

BREAD BOARD

30

Materials Required

Part	Number	Size	Material
handle	1	¾ " x 3¼ " x 12 "	walnut or birch
board	1	½ " x 6 " x 17 "	pine or maple
wood screws	2	#9, 1¼ " flathead	
dowel plugs	2	⅜ " dia. x 1½ "	birch
glue			

Bread Board Plans

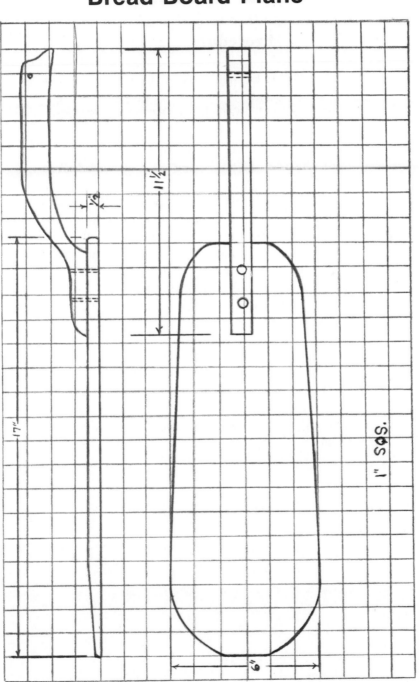

BREAD BOARD

Procedure

1. Lay out and cut both pieces to the suggested size and shape indicated. Use a plane to bevel the front of the board, then shape the handle by rounding the edges with a half–round file. If the rectangular board is chosen, use a plane to make a ½–inch chamfer at a 45–degree angle on top of the board.
2. Locate and drill two countersunk pilot holes through the bottom of the board and into the handle, then fasten the handle to the board with #9, 1¼–inch plathead wood screws. An alternative procedure to fastening the handle is to bore two ⅜–inch diameter holes through the handle and board, then to insert two ⅜–inch dowel plugs into the holes with glue.
3. Locate and drill a ³⁄₁₆–inch diameter hole through the handle for hanging the board.
4. Scrape all traces of glue, then sand the bread board to a smooth surface.
5. Apply several coats of clear oil finish, rubbing between coats with fine steel wool or pumice and lemon oil.

COAT RACK

31

Materials Required

Part	Number	Size	Material
base	2	2½" x 2½" x 17"	pine or the wood of your choice
brace	4	¾" x 3" x 6"	
hook	4	¾" x 3" x 6"	
center post	1	2" x 2" x 16"	
wood screw	12	#10, 1½" flathead	
wood screw	1	#14, 4" flathead	

Coat Rack Plans

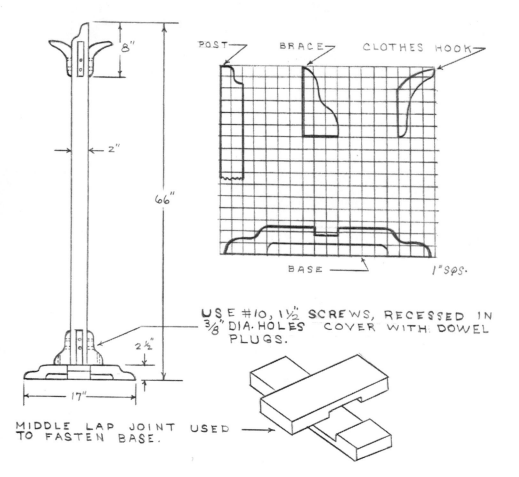

MIDDLE LAP JOINT USED
TO FASTEN BASE.

Procedure

1. Lay out and cut the stock to the size and design indicated on the drawing.
2. Lay out and cut a half lap joint into the two base pieces. Fasten the base together by gluing and clamping the two pieces into the half lap joint.
3. Drill a pilot hole through the center of the base

COAT RACK

and center post, then proceed to attach the center post to the base with a large screw.

4. Drill three ⅜–inch counterbored pilot holes into each brace, then fasten the four braces to the centerpost and base with #10, 1½–inch flathead wood screws. Cover all screw holes with ⅜–inch niture buttons.

5. Drill two ⅜–inch counterbored pilot holes into each coat hook then fasten the four coat hooks to the top of the center post with #10, 1½–inch flathead wood screws. Cover all screw holes with furniture buttons.

6. Clean all traces of glue, then sand the project to a smooth surface.

7. Select and apply the colored stain or paint of your choice. When dry, apply several coats of clear polyurethane finish, rubbing between each coat with fine steel wool or pumice and oil. To protect the finish apply a coat of paste wax and buff.

SERVING BOARD

32

Materials Required

Part	Number	Size	Material
strip	8	½" x 1⅛" x 10"	mahogany
strip	8	½" x 1⅛" x 10"	maple
waterproof glue			

Note: The pieces are cut to a 10″ length to allow for waste due to the saw kerf.

Serving Board Plans

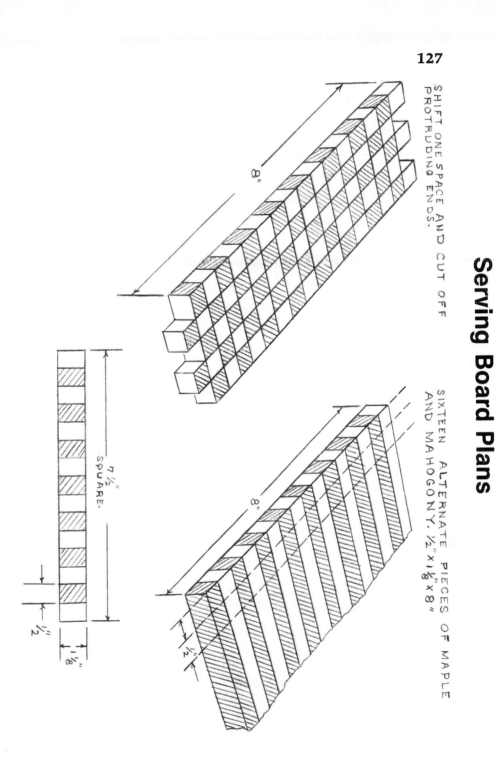

SHIFT ONE SPACE AND CUT OFF PROTRUDING ENDS.

8"

SIXTEEN ALTERNATE PIECES OF MAPLE AND MAHOGONY. ½" x 1⅛" x 8"

8"

½"

7½" SQUARE.

½"

1⅛"

SERVING BOARD

Procedure

1. Lay out and cut sixteen ½ x 1⅛ x 8–inch strips. Eight of the strips should be mahogany or walnut and eight of the strips should be maple or birch.
2. Glue and clamp the sixteen alternate strips together, making sure that all of the glue joints are clamped tight.
3. Scrape away all traces of glue, then proceed to plane the top and bottom surfaces smooth.
4. Set the saw for a ½–inch cut, then make fifteen cuts across the glued–up board. (Refer to drawing).
5. Glue and clamp the fifteen ½ x 8–inch strips together, making sure to shift one space for each strip. (Refer to drawing).
6. Cut off the protruding ends. (Refer to drawing).
7. Scrape all traces of glue, then plane both surfaces even.
8. Sand the board to a smooth surface, then apply several coats of finishing oil. Rub between each coat with fine steel wool.

LAZY SUSAN

33

Materials Required

Part	Number	Size	Material
round tray	1	⅝" x 16" dia.	pine or the wood of your choice
base	1	1" x 8½" x 8½"	
bearing mechanism	1	4" x 4"	
wood screws	8	#6, ½" flathead	

Note: The bearing mechanism can be purchased at a local hard ware store.

Procedure

1. Edge–glue the stock to reach the recommended width.
2. Lay out and cut all stock to the suggested size and design.

Lazy Susan Plans

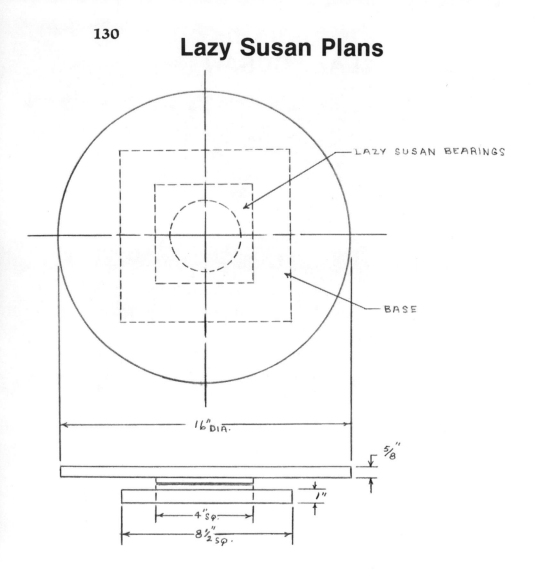

LAZY SUSAN BEARINGS

BASE

16" DIA.

5/8"

1"

4" SQ.

8½" SQ.

3. The edge of the lazy susan is equally attractive if it is left alone or if there is a cove cut routed around.

4. Fasten the lazy susan bearing mechanism to the center of the base and tray bottom. Use #6, ½–inch flathead screws.

5. Sand the entire project to a smooth surface. Select and apply a stain of your choice. When thoroughly dry, apply several coats of finishing oil, rubbing lightly between each coat with fine steel wool or pumice and oil.

WINE RACK

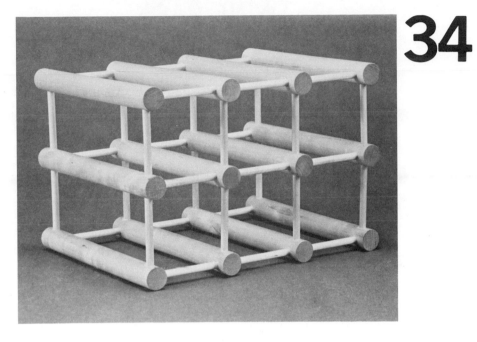

34

Materials Required

Part	Number	Size	Material
dowels	12	1¼ " x 12 "	birch
dowels	16	⅜ " x 5¼ "	birch
dowels	6	⅜ " x 12 "	birch

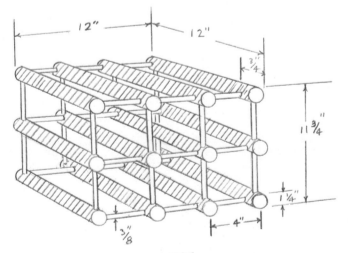

WINE RACK

Procedure

1. Lay out and cut all of the dowels to the suggested size.
2. Construct the three horizontal levels first. Drill ⅜–inch diameter holes halfway through the ends of the two 12 x 1¼–inch diameter dowels and completely through the two center dowels. Be sure to use a spade bit and to make sure that the three levels are aligned perfectly. To avoid wood chipping when drilling, drill from one side until the bit point sticks out, then turn and complete the hole from the opposite side.
3. Insert the ⅜ x 12–inch dowels into the joints, using glue to fasten them. Be sure the levels are completely aligned.
4. Locate and drill thirty-two ⅜–inch diameter holes to a depth of ½ inch to receive the vertical dowels. Drill into both sides of the middle level and into one side of the top level and one side of the bottom level.
5. Insert the eight vertical dowels into the bottom level, then continue to press the middle level onto these ⅜–inch dowels.
6. Insert the remaining dowels into the top of the middle level holes and continue in the same procedure as step five.
7. Before the glue dries, check with a framing square to see if the wine rack is aligned at right angles.
8. Sand the entire rack to a smooth surface.
9. Select and apply the paint or stain of your choice.
10. Apply several coats of oil or polyurethane, rubbing between coats with fine steel wool or pumice and oil.

MEMO HOLDER

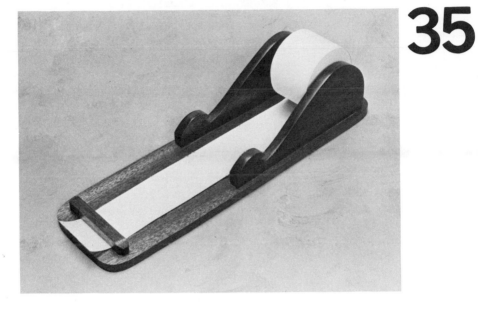

Materials Required

Part	Number	Size	Material
back	1	½ " x 4¾ " x 16"	mahogany or the wood of your choice
side	2	½ " x 3½ " x 8½ "	
paper cutter	1	½ " x ½ " x 4"	
dowel	1	⅜ " x 3¾ "	
glue			
wood screws	4	#6, 1¼ " flathead	

Note: Adding machine paper is available at your local stationary store.

Memo Holder Plans

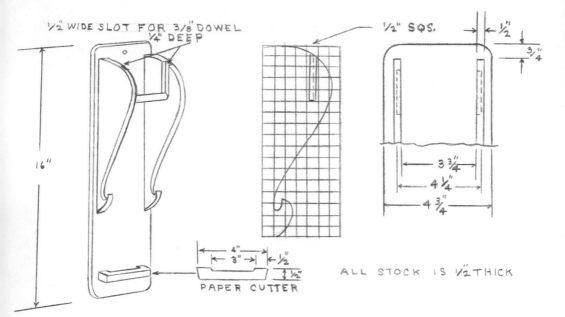

Procedure

1. Lay out and cut the back and side pieces to the size and design indicated. Lay out and chisel cut the two ¼ x ½-inch slots into the side pieces.
2. Lay out and cut the two ends of the paper cutter to 15-degree angle. File approximately ¹⁄₁₆-inch depth into the bottom of the paper cutter to produce a slot to receive the paper. Fasten the paper cutter to the back by gluing and clamping.
3. Attach the side pieces to the back by drilling two countersunk pilot holes into each side, then fastening the pieces together with #6, 1¼-inch flathead wood screws.
4. Cut a ⅜ x 3¾-inch birch dowel to hold the roll of paper.
5. At the top center, drill a ³⁄₁₆-inch hole to hang the memo holder.
6. Select and apply the stain or paint of your choice. When dry, apply several coats of clear finishing oil, rubbing between each coat with fine steel wool or pumice and oil. Protect the finish with a coat and paste wax and buff.
7. Insert the ⅜-inch dowel through the roll of paper and into the two slots.

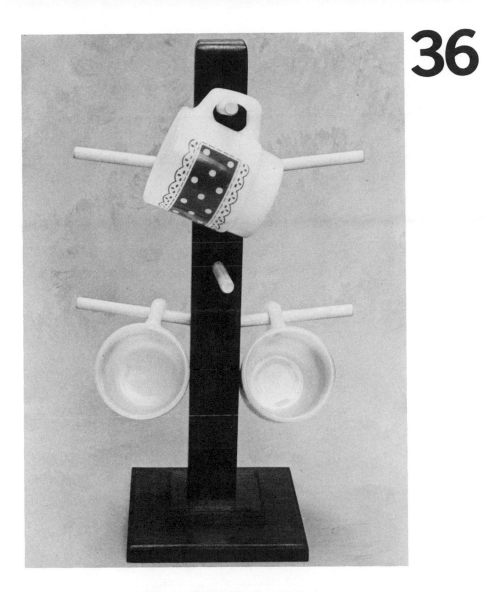

Materials Required

Part	Number	Size	Material
post	1	1½ " x 1½ " x 16 "	pine or the wood of your choice
dowel	8	⅜ " dia. x 4 "	
dowel pin	1	½ " dia. x 1⅞ "	
base, top	1	½ " x 3 " x 3 "	
base, bottom	1	½ " x 6 " x 6 "	
glue			

Mug Tree Plans

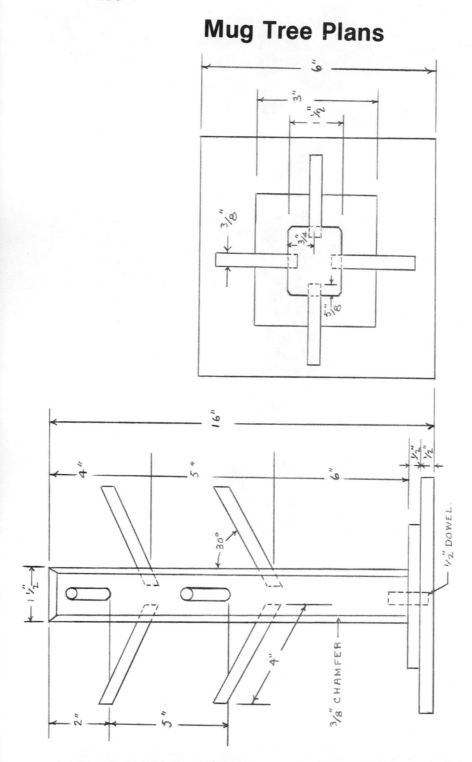

MUG TREE

Procedure

1. Lay out and cut all pieces to the size indicated in the drawing.
2. Lay out and cut a ⅜–inch chamfer on the four edges of the post. The chamfered cuts may extend to the full length of the post or they can stop 1 inch from either end of the post.
3. Lay out and bore the eight ⅜–inch diameter holes into the post, using a sliding T-bevel to assure the correct 30–degree angle. Insert the eight ⅜ x 4–inch dowels into the holes with glue.
4. Assemble the base pieces together by gluing and clamping. For added design to the base use a chamfer or cove cut around both squares.
5. Bore a ½ x 1–inch hole through the bottom of the post. Bore a ½ x ⅞–inch hole through the center of the base. Fasten the post to the base with a ½ x 1⅞–inch dowel pin inserted into the two bored holes with glue.
6. Scrape all traces of glue, then sand the mug tree to a smooth surface.
7. Select and apply the stain or paint of your choice. When dry, apply several coats of clear polyurethane finish, rubbing between coats with fine steel wool or pumice and oil. Protect the finish by applying a coat of paste wax and buffing.

TOWEL RACK CABINET

37

Materials Required

Part	Number	Size	Material
back	1	¾" x 11½" x 29½"	cherry or the wood of your choice
side	2	¾" x 8" x 16"	
top shelf	1	¾" x 7¼" x 28"	
bottom shelf	1	¾" x 7¼" x 28"	
drawer			
divider	1	¾" x 4" 7¼"	
dowel	1	½" x 29½"	birch
knob	2	¾" dia.	wood or brass

Drawer parts:

front	2	¾" x 3¹⁵⁄₁₆" x 13½"	
side	4	⅜" x 3¹⁵⁄₁₆" x 7"	
back	2	⅜" x 3¹⁵⁄₁₆" x 12¾"	
bottom	2	⅜" x 6¼" x 12¾"	
nails		#6 finishing	
brads		1" finishing	
glue			

Towel Rack Cabinet Plans

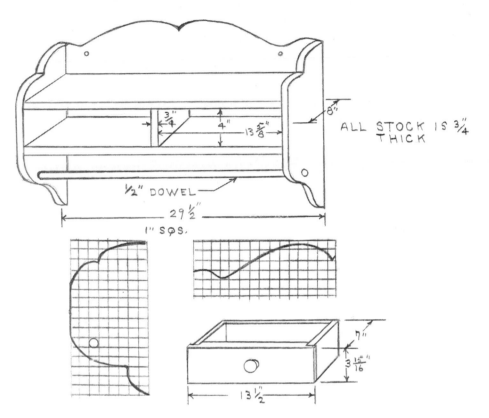

Procedure

1. Lay out and cut all pieces to the suggested size and design.
2. Bore two ½–inch holes into the side pieces, then insert the ½–inch dowel with glue.
3. Fasten the top shelf and bottom piece to the sides and back using #6 finishing nails. Locate the center, then attach the drawer divider by gluing and clamping.
4. Lay out and cut the ¼ x ⅜–inch rabbet joints on the two front pieces, then proceed to assemble the

TOWEL RACK CABINET

drawers to the size suggested, using 1–inch finishing brads.

5. Attach the two pull knobs to the center of each drawer.

6. Drill two $\frac{3}{16}$–inch holes 16 inches apart to hang the towel rack.

7. Set and fill all nail holes, then sand the project to a smooth surface.

8. Select and apply the stain or paint of your choice. When dry, apply several coats of clear poly-urethane finish, rubbing between each coat with fine steel wool or pumice oil. To preserve the finish apply a coat of paste wax and buff.

LAMINATED DESK SET

38

Materials Required

Part	Number	Size	Material
strip	12	2" x ³/₁₆" x 9½"	maple
strip	12	½" x ³/₁₆" x 9½"	walnut
letter holder	1	1" x 1½" x 3"	walnut or maple
pen funnel and pen	1		

Note: Pen available at local stationery store.

Laminated Desk Set Plans

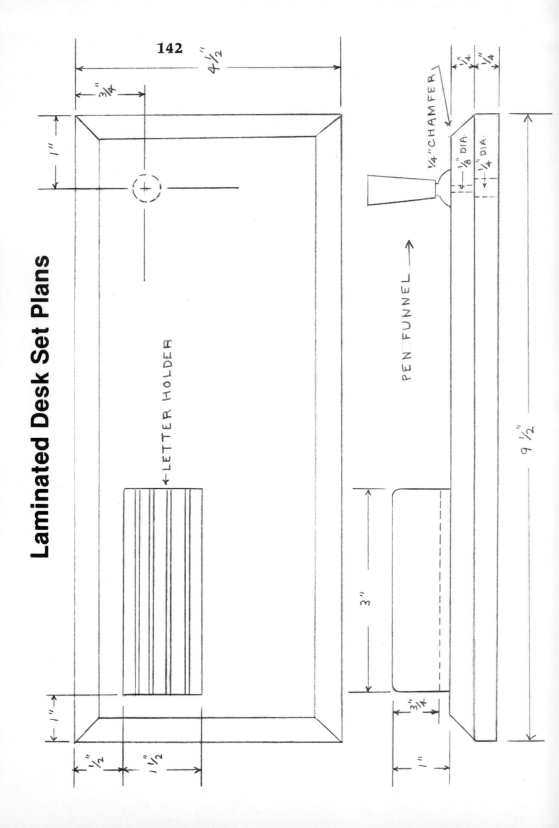

142

4½"

3/4"

1"

LETTER HOLDER

½"

1½"

1"

¼" CHAMFER

¼"   ¼"

⅛" DIA.

¼" DIA.

PEN FUNNEL →

9½"

3"

3/4"

1"

LAMINATED DESK SET

Procedure

1. Cut the twenty-four strips to the size and material indicated.
2. Plane the edges smooth, then glue up and clamp the twenty-four alternate strips.
3. Plane the surfaces even, then proceed to lay out and cut a ¼–inch chamfer.
4. Construct the letter–holding block by setting the saw for a ¾–inch depth, then make four cuts on the block approximately ⁵⁄₁₆ of an inch apart. The saw cut is ⅛–inch wide and is used for a slot to hold letters or papers. Plane the bottom of the letter holder to approximately a 10–degree angle so that the block is fastened at a slight angle to the base.
5. Fasten the letter holder to the base by gluing and clamping.
6. Locate and drill a countersunk pilot hole through the bottom of the base for the open funnel.
7. Sand the project to a smooth surface, then apply several coats of clear finishing oil, rubbing between coats with fine steel wool or pumice and lemon oil. Protect the surface by applying a coat of paste wax and buff.
8. Attach the pen funnel to the base by threading the swivel funnel onto the threaded stud.

UTILITY BOX

Materials Required

Part	Number	Size	Material
back decorative piece	1	½ " x 2 " x 14 "	cherry or the wood of your choice
back	1	½ " x 10 " x 14 "	
side	2	½ " x 5 ¾ " x 10 "	
top	1	½ " x 1 ½ " x 14 "	
lid	1	½ " x 6 " x 14 "	
shelf	1	½ " x 5 " x 13 "	
bottom	1	½ " x 5 " x 13 "	
front	1	½ " x 3 ¼ " x 14 "	

Drawer parts

front	1	¾ " x 3¹¹⁄₁₆ " x 14 "	
side	2	⅜ " x 3¹¹⁄₁₆ " x 4⅞ "	
back	1	⅜ " x 3¹¹⁄₁₆ " x 12⅜ "	
bottom	1	⅜ " x 4⅝ " x 12⅜ "	
butt hinge	2	⅛ " x 1 "	
knob	1	½ " dia. porcelain	
nails		#4 finishing	

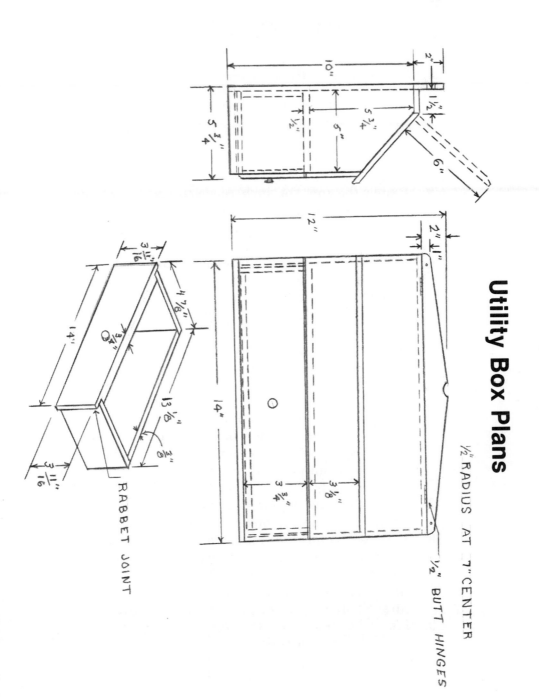

Utility Box Plans

½ RADIUS AT 7" CENTER

½ BUTT HINGES

RABBET JOINT

UTILITY BOX

Procedure

1. Lay out and cut all pieces to the suggested size and design.
2. Fasten the sides to the back, then fasten the shelf and the bottom to the sides. Use #4 finishing nails and glue.
3. Fasten the top 1½-inch piece to the top of the sides, then attach the back decorative piece to the back edge of the top piece. Use glue and #4 finishing nails.
4. Cut the top edge of the front piece to a 45-degree angle and proceed to fasten the front to the side pieces using #4 finishing nails and glue. Also cut the front and back edge of the lid to a 45-degree angle.
5. Lay out and cut four ⅛ x 1-inch gains to receive the 1-inch butt hinges. Attach the two 1-inch butt hinges to the lid and top edges using #4, ⅜-inch flathead screws.
6. Construct the drawer to the dimensions given. The rabbet joint on the front piece should be ¼ x ⅞ inches; the ½-inch extension of the joint will allow the front of the drawer to fit flush with the front of the box.
7. Clean all traces of glue, set and fill all holes, then proceed to sand the box to a smooth surface.
8. Select and apply the colored stain or paint of your choice. When dry, apply several coats of clear polyurethane finish. Rub between each coat with fine steel wool or pumice and oil. To protect the surace apply a coat of paste wax and buff.
9. Find the center of the drawer and attach a ¾-inch brass or wood knob.

PENCIL HOLDER

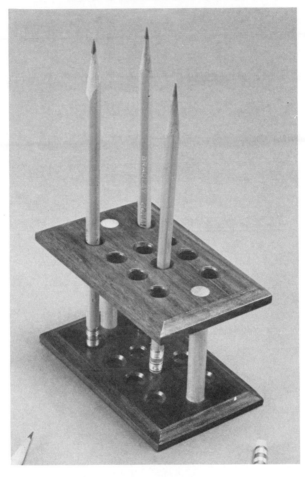

Materials Required

Part	Number	Size	Material
top	1	⅜" x 2¾" x 4½"	walnut
base	1	⅜" x 2¾" x 4½"	walnut
dowel	2	⅜" dia. x 2⅞"	
glue			

147

Pencil Holder Plans

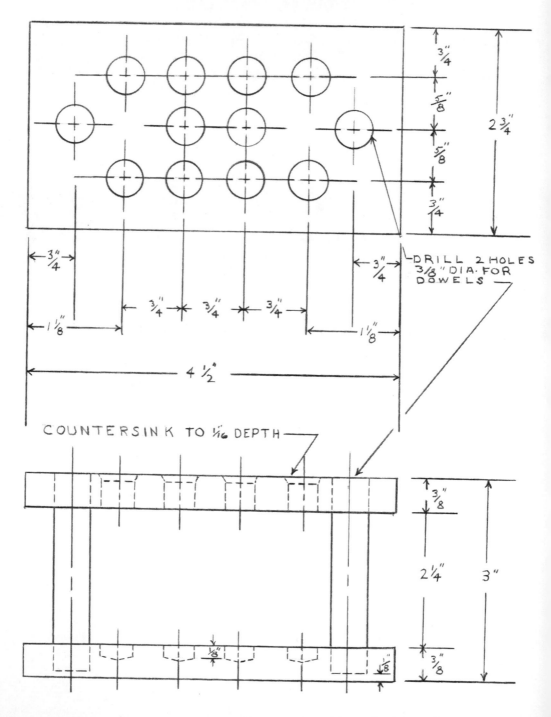

PENCIL HOLDER

Procedure

1. Lay out and cut the top and base pieces to the size indicated.
2. Tape the top piece onto the base piece, then lay out the points to be drilled. Drill the twelve $3/8$–inch holes through the top and into the bottom piece to a $1/8$–inch depth.
3. Use a $3/4$–inch drill to countersink to a depth of $1/16$ of an inch on all $3/8$–inch holes.
4. Cut two $3/8$–inch diameter dowels to the size indicated, then sand all of the pieces to a smooth surface before assembly.
5. Assemble the pencil holder by inserting the two dowels into the $3/8$–inch holes with glue. Clean all traces of glue.
6. When thoroughly sanded, apply several coats of clear polyurethane finish, rubbing between coats with fine steel wool or pumice and oil. Protect the finish by applying a coat of wax and buffing.

MATCH BOX HOLDER

41

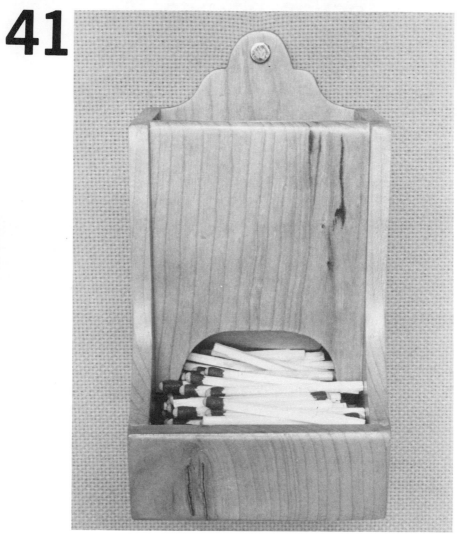

Materials Required

Part	Number	Size	Material
back	1	¼" x 3¼" x 7⅜"	birch or the wood of your choice
side	2	¼" x 3" x 5"	
front	1	¼" x 3¼" x 1½"	
bottom	1	¼" x 3" x 2¾"	
front	1	¼" x 3¼" x 3¾"	
brads		¾" finishing	
glue			

Match Box Holder Plans

¼ SQS

TOP IS LEFT OPEN TO
RECEIV MATCH BOX

ALL STOCK IS
¼" THICK.

1½"

7¼"

5"

1 ¼" R.

⅜"

2¼"

3½"

¾

2 ½"

3 ¾"

2 ½" R

1 ¼"

1"

1 ¼"

3 ¼"

3 ¾"

¼"

Procedure

1. Lay out and cut all pieces to the suggested size and design.
2. Fasten the sides to the back using glue and ¾–inch finishing brads. Fasten the two front pieces to the sides, then attach the bottom, using glue and ¾–inch finishing brads.
3. Locate and drill two holes into the top and bottom of the back piece.
4. Scrape all traces of glue, set and fill all nail holes,

MATCH BOX HOLDER

then proceed to sand the project to a smooth surface.

5. Select and apply the stain or paint of your choice. When dry, apply several coats of clear oil finish, rubbing between coats with fine ateel wool or pumice and oil. Protect the finish with a coat of paste wax and buff.

ALBUM/BOOK RACK

Materials Required

Part	Number	Size	Material
sides	2	¾" x 8" x 12"	walnut or hardwood of your choice
rails	2	½" x 3" x 20"	

Album/Book Rack Plans

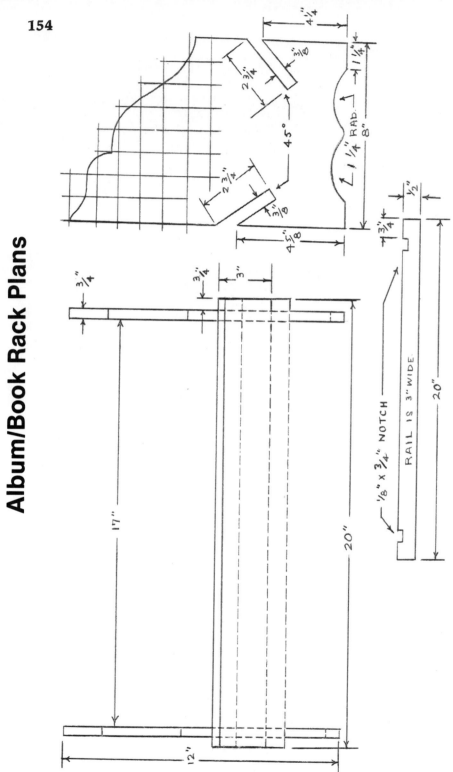

ALBUM/BOOK RACK

Procedure

1. Lay out and cut all materials to the size and design indicated in the drawing.
2. Cut the ⅜ x 2¾–inch slots in the two sides to receive the rails.
3. Cut two ¾–inch blind dado joints to form the notches in each rail. The depth should be ⅛ inch; the length should be 2¾ inches. The blind dados can be cut on the table saw with a dado cutter; then they should be trimmed with a chisel.
4. Fasten the rails to the sides by applying glue to the dado notches, then slide the notches into the cut–out slots in each side piece.
5. Clean all traces of glue and sand the album rack to a smooth surface.
6. Apply several coats of clear lacquer or polyurethane. Rub between each coat with fine steel wool or pumice and oil. To preserve the finish apply a coat of paste wax, and then buff.

WALL SHELF I

43

Materials Required

Part	Number	Size	Material
side	2	¾ " x 6½ " x 25½ "	walnut or the wood of your choice
top shelf	1	¾ " x 4⅜ " x 24¼ "	
middle shelf	1	¾ " x 5½ " x 24¼ "	
bottom shelf	1	¾ " x 6½ " x 24½ "	
leather strip, for hanging shelf	1	⅛ " x ¼ " x 30 "	
glue			

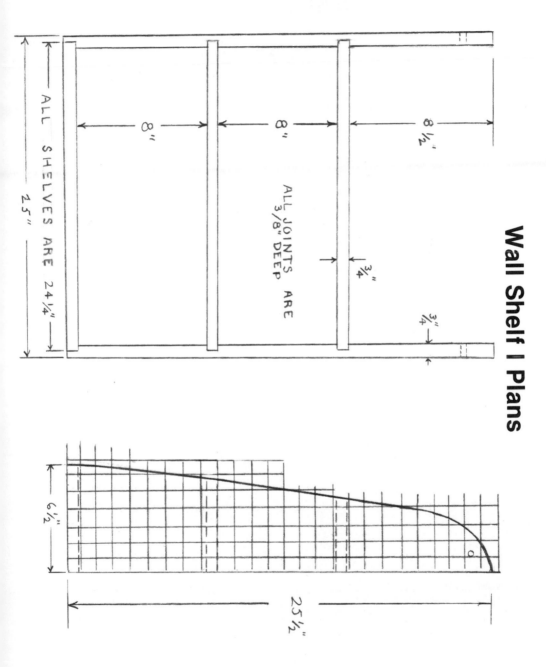

Wall Shelf I Plans

25"

ALL SHELVES ARE 24¼"

8"

8"

8½"

ALL JOINTS ARE
3/8" DEEP

3/4"

3/4"

6½"

25½"

WALL SHELF I

Procedure

1. Lay out and cut all pieces to the suggested size and design.
2. Lay out and cut the dado and rabbet joints to a depth of $\frac{3}{8}$ inches.
3. Assemble the shelves to the sides by gluing and clamping.
4. Plane the protruding edges of the shelves even to the sides of the wall shelf.
5. Drill two $\frac{1}{4}$-inch holes through the sides to hang the shelf.
6. Scrape all traces of glue, then sand the wall shelf to a smooth surface.
7. Select and apply the stain or paint of your choice. When dry, apply several coats of clear finishing oil, rubbing between coats with fine steel wool or pumice and oil. Protect the finish by applying a coat of paste wax and buffing.

WALL SHELF II

44

Materials Required

Part	Number	Size	Material
shelf	1	¾ ″ x 9½ ″ x 30″	pine or the wood of your choice
bracket	2	¾ ″ x 7″ x 9″	
back	1	¾ ″ x 2″ x 30″	
wood screws		4	#8, 1½ ″ flathead

Wall Shelf II Plans

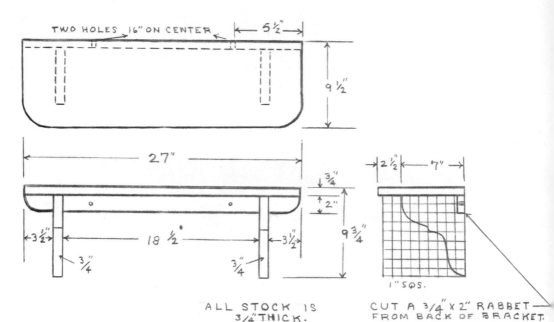

TWO HOLES 16" ON CENTER — 5½" — 9½"

27" — ¾" — 2" — 9¾"

←3½→ — 18½ — ←3½→ — ¾

2½ — 7"

ALL STOCK IS 3/4" THICK.

1" SQS.

CUT A 3/4" X 2" RABBET FROM BACK OF BRACKET.

Procedure

1. Lay out and cut all pieces to the suggested size and design.
2. Lay out and cut the ¾ x 2–inch rabbet on the back of the bracket pieces.
3. Assemble the back piece into the cut rabbet joints in the brackets by drilling pilot and countersink holes, then fastening two wood screws into each bracket. Fasten the top piece to the brackets and back by gluing and clamping.
4. Drill two ³⁄₁₆–inch diameter holes exactly 16 inches apart into the back pieces. The holes are located so they are aligned to the studs in a wall for hanging the shelf.
5. Clean all traces of glue, set and fill all nail holes, then sand the shelf to a smooth surface.
6. Select and apply the colored stain or paint of your choice. When dry, apply several coats of clear polyurethane, rubbing lightly between each coat with fine steel wool or pumice and oil. Protect the finish by applying paste wax and buffing.

WALL SHELF III

Materials Required

Part	Number	Size	Material
back	1	½" x 8¼" x 11"	mahogany or the wood of your choice
side	2	½" x 6" x 6"	
bottom	1	½" x 6" 10"	
nails		#4 finishing	
glue			

Wall Shelf III Plans

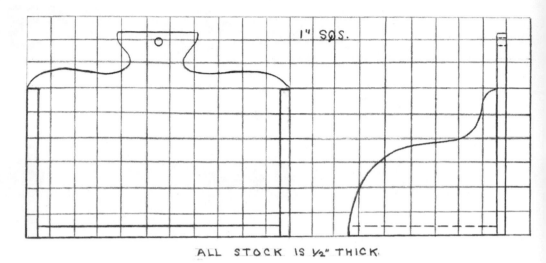

ALL STOCK IS ½" THICK.

Procedure

1. Lay out and cut all pieces to the suggested size and design.
2. Fasten the two sides and bottom to the back by gluing and nailing with #4 finishing nails.
3. Scrape all glue, set and fill all nail holes, then sand the shelf to a smooth surface.
4. Select and apply the stain or paint of your choice. When dry, apply several coats of clear oil finish, rubbing between coats with fine steel wool or pumice and oil. Protect the finish by applying a coat of paste wax and buffing.

TIE RACK SHIELD

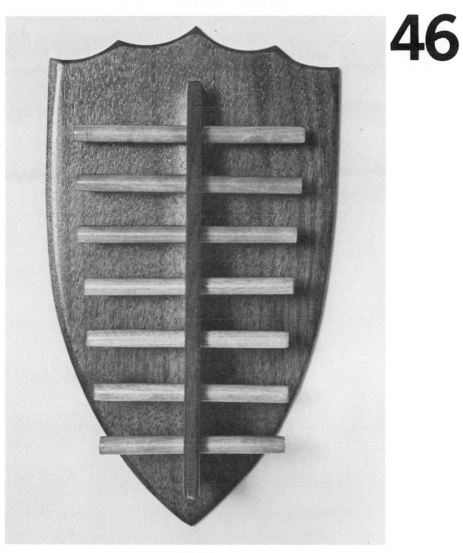

Materials Required

Part	Number	Size	Material
back	1	³⁄₈" x 6" x 9¹⁵⁄₁₆"	walnut or the wood of your choice
bracket	1	³⁄₈" x 4½" x 8⁵⁄₁₆"	
dowel	1	³⁄₈" dia. x 36"	
wood screws	3	#5, ¾" flathead	
glue			

Tie Rack Shield Plans

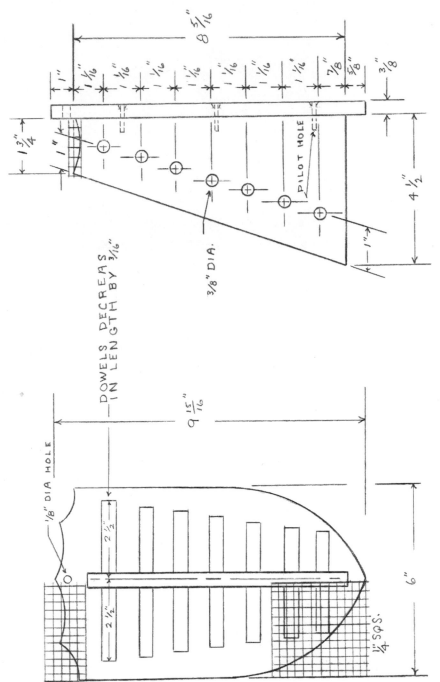

5/16"
8"
1" 1/16" 1/16" 1/16" 1/16" 1/16" 1/16" 1/16" 7/8" 5/8"
3/8"
1 3/4"
1"
PILOT HOLE
4 1/2"
1"
DOWELS DECREAS IN LENGTH BY 3/16"
3/8" DIA.
9 15/16"
1/8" DIA HOLE
2 1/2"
2 1/2"
6"
1/4" SQS.

TIE RACK SHIELD

Procedure

1. Lay out and cut the shield and bracket to the suggested size and shape.
2. Lay out and bore the seven $\frac{3}{8}$–inch diameter holes through the bracket piece.
3. Lay out and cut the seven $\frac{3}{8}$–inch diameter dowels. Start with a 5–inch length and reduce the length of each following dowel by $\frac{3}{16}$ of an inch. Fasten the seven dowels into the bored holes with glue.
4. Mark and drill three pilot and countersink holes through the back and into the bracket. Fasten the bracket to the back with wood screws.
5. Drill a $\frac{1}{8}$–inch diameter hole into the top of the shield for hanging the tie rack.
6. Clean all traces of glue, then sand the project to a smooth surface.
7. Select and apply the colored stain or paint of your choice. When dry, apply several coats of clear polyurethane finish. Rub between each coat with fine steel wool or pumice and oil. Protect the finish with a coat of paste wax.

SALT / PEPPER SHAKERS

Materials Required

Part	Number	Size	Material
block	2	1½" x 1" x 3½"	walnut, maple, or the wood of your choice
cork	2	¾" taper	

Note: The cork may be purchased at your local hardware or craft supply store.

Salt / Pepper Shakers Plans

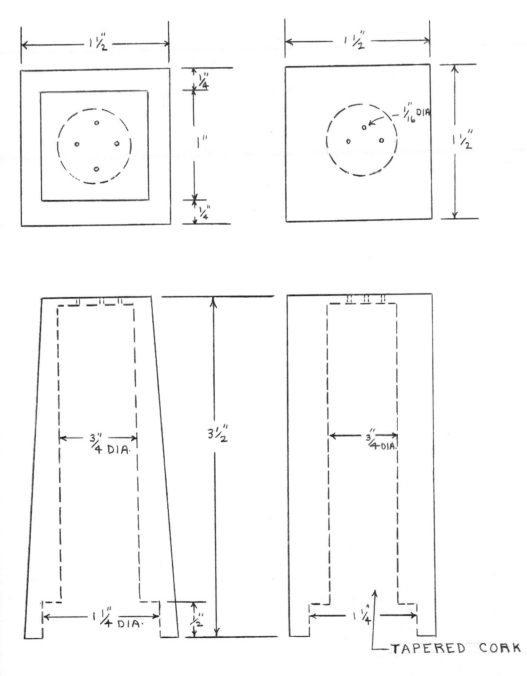

SALT/PEPPER SHAKERS

Procedure

1. Lay out and cut the pieces to the size and design selected from the drawing.
2. Use a spade bit to bore a 1¼–inch diameter hole to a ½–inch depth through the bottom of the stock. With a ¾–inch twist drill bore a second hole through the bottom of the stock to a depth of $3\frac{5}{16}$ inches.
3. Lay out and drill the correct number of $\frac{1}{16}$–inch holes on the top of the shakers.
4. Sand the shakers to a smooth surface, then apply the stain or paint of your choice. When dry, apply several coats of clear finishing oil, rubbing between each coat with fine steel wool or pumice oil. Protect the finish by applying a coat of paste wax and buffing.
5. Fill the shakers and insert the ¾–inch tapered cork.

MIRRORS

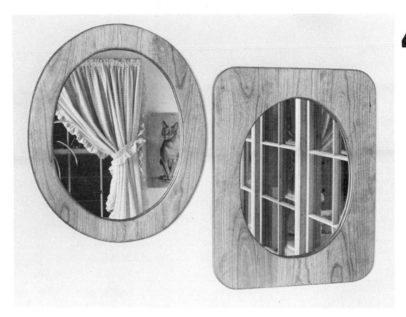

48

Materials Required

Part	Number	Size	Material
Oval frame:			
frame	1	¾ " x 15 " x 20 "	pine or the wood of your choice
oval mirror	1	⅛" x 10½ " x 16 "	
Rectangular frame:			
frame	1	¾ " x 15 " x 21 "	pine or the wood of your choice
oval mirror	1	⅛" x 9" x 15 "	

Note: The oval mirror can be cut to your pattern at a local glass supply store. Oval mirrors can also be purchased pre-cut.

Mirrors Plans

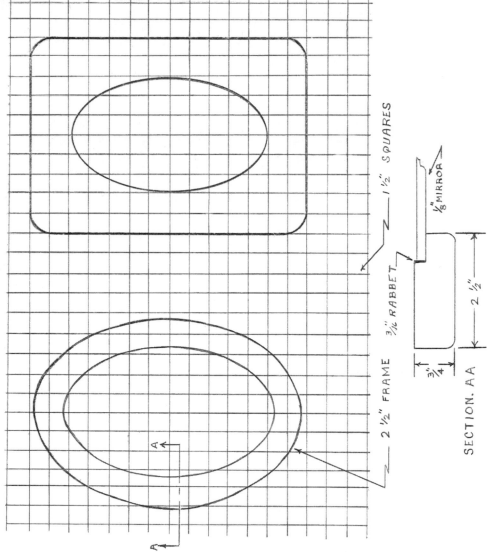

1 ½" SQUARES

3/16" RABBET

2 ½" FRAME

⅛" MIRROR

2 ½"

¾"

SECTION. AA

MIRRORS

Procedure

1. Glue up and clamp the stock to the required width. Select and lay out the design of the mirror on the glued–up board.
2. Cut the board to the selected design. To cut the oval design out bore a ⅜–inch diameter hole, then insert the blade of a sabre saw to do the cutting.
3. With a router and rabbet bit, cut a ³⁄₁₆ x ⅜–inch rabbet recess on the back side of the oval cut–out to receive the oval mirror.
4. Scrape all traces of glue; file and sand the frame to a smooth surface.
5. Select and apply the stain or paint of your choice. When dry, apply several coats of clear polyurethane finish, rubbing between coats with fine steel wool or pumice and oil. To protect the finish apply a coat of paste wax and buff.
6. Fasten the mirror into the rabbet recess with glass points placed approximately 5 inches apart.

RECITE BOX

49

Materials Required

Part	Number	Size	Material
top	1	½ " x 6¾ " x 6¾ "	pine or the wood of your choice
side	2	½ " x 5" x 8"	
back	1	½ " x 5" x 6⁵⁄₁₆ "	
bottom	1	½ " x 4½ " x 5"	
front	1	½ " x 6½ " x 6"	
dowel pin	2	¼ " x 1"	
nails		#4 finishing	

Recipe Box Plans

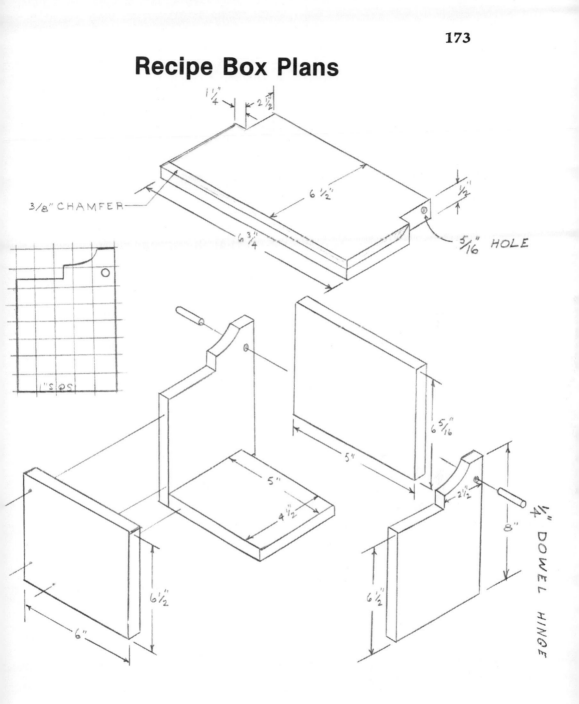

1 1/4" 2 1/2"

3/8" CHAMFER

6 1/2"

6 3/4"

1/2"

5/16" HOLE

1 SQ."

5 1/16"

5"

5"

4 1/2"

2 1/2"

8"

6 1/2"

6 1/2"

6"

1/4" DOWEL HINGE

RECIPE BOX

Procedure

1. Lay out and cut all stock to the suggested size and design.
2. Fasten the two sides, and the bottom, back, and front together, using glue and #4 finishing nails. Be sure that the back piece is fastened $\frac{3}{16}$ of an inch lower than the top so that the lid has clear-
3. ance to open.
4. Lay out and cut the $\frac{3}{8}$–inch chamfer on the top lid.
5. Lay out points and bore the two $\frac{5}{16}$–inch diameter holes into the edge of the lid. Lay out points and drill the two $\frac{1}{4}$–inch diameter holes into the side pieces.
6. Cut the two $\frac{1}{4}$ x 1–inch dowel pins and proceed to fasten the top to the sides by inserting the dowel pins through the sides and into the lid edge.
7. Set and fill all nail holes. Sand the box to a smooth surface. Select and apply the stain of your choice.
8. When dry, apply several coats of polyurethane finish. Rub between coats with fine steel wool or pumice and oil. Protect the finish with paste wax.

PIPE STAND

50

Materials Required

Part	Number	Size	Material
handle	1	⅝ " x 1½ " x 2 "	cherry or the wood of your choice
top design	1	˙ ⅜ " x 6" dia.	
base design	1	½ " x 7" dia.	
center post			
dowel	1	1¼ " dia. x 3½ "	
dowel pin	2	⅜ " x 1½ "	

175

Pipe Stand Plans

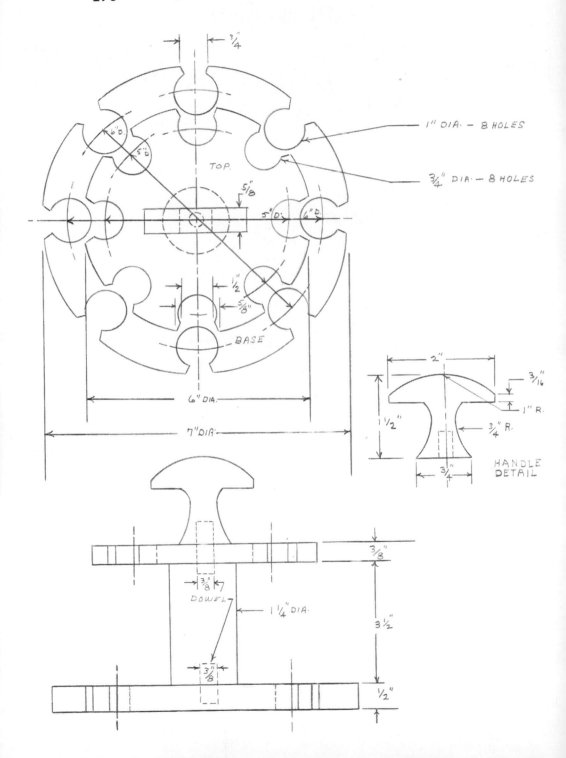

PIPE STAND

Procedure

1. Lay out and cut the ½ x 7–inch diameter base. Lay out and bore the eight 1–inch diameter holes around the perimeter of the base.
2. Lay out and cut the ⅜ x 6–inch diameter top. Lay out and bore the eight ¾–inch diameter holes around the perimeter of the top.
3. Cut the 1¼–inch diameter dowel to length, making sure both ends are cut square.
4. Lay out and cut the handle to the design in the drawing.
5. Lay out and bore a ⅜–inch diameter hole to a ½–inch depth into the base of the handle. Continue to bore the same hole completely through the center of the top piece. Bore a ⅜–inch diameter hole completely through the center of the bottom piece and continue to bore the same hole to a ½–inch depth through both ends of the 1¼–inch diameter center dowel.
6. Cut the dowel pins to length and continue to fasten the pipe stand together using glue.
7. Select and apply the stain of your choice. When dry, apply several coats of clear lacquer. Rub between coats with fine steel wool. Protect the finish with a coat of paste wax, buff.

REFLECTION SHELF

Materials Required

Part	Number	Size	Material
back	1	½ " x 7" x 11½ "	pine or the wood of your choice
side	2	½ " x 5½ " x 10"	
bottom	1	½ " x 6" x 7½ "	
mirror	1	⅛ " x 6" x 8"	
nails		#4 finishing	
glass points			
glue			

Note: Your local glass supply store will cut the mirror to the size pattern you desire. Mirrors can be purchased pre-cut from a craft supply store.

Reflection Shelf Plans

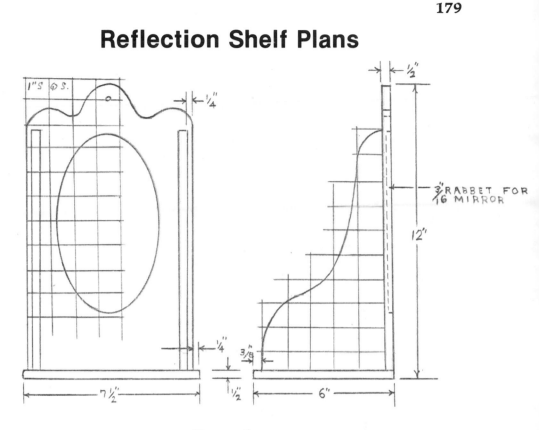

Procedure

1. Lay out and cut all pieces to the suggested size and design.
2. With a router and rabbet bit cut a $^3/_{16}$ x $^3/_8$–inch recess on the back side of the oval design.
3. Fasten the two sides to the back, then fasten the bottom to the sides and back. Use glue and #4 finishing nails.
4. Scrape all traces of glue, set and fill all nail holes, then proceed to sand the sconce to a smooth surface.
5. Select and apply the stain or paint of your choice. When dry, apply several coats of clear finishing oil, rubbing between coats with fine steel wool or pumice and oil. Protect the surface with a coat of paste wax and buff.
6. Fasten the oval mirror into the rabbet recess with glass points located approximately 2 inches apart.

CORNER SHELF

52

Materials Required

Part	Number	Size	Material
side	2	½" x 6" x 17½"	cherry or the wood of your choice
top shelf	1	½" x 3" x 6"	
middle shelf	1	½" x 3¾" x 7½"	
bottom shelf	1	½" x 4¾" x 9"	
nails		#4 finishing	
glue			

SCREW HOLE.

MITER JOINT

TOP 3" R.

MIDDLE 3¾" R.

BOTTOM 4½" R.

Corner Shelf Plans

CORNER SHELF

Procedure

1. Lay out and cut the two side pieces to ½ x 6 x 17½ inches. Set the saw to a 45–degree angle and continue to cut the 45–degree miter joint on one edge of each piece.
2. Lay out and cut the design on the sides and shelves.
3. Fasten the two sides by gluing and nailing into the miter joint with #4 finishing nails.
4. Assemble the three shelves to the sides by gluing and nailing with #4 finishing nails.
5. Drill two $\frac{3}{16}$–inch diameter holes through the sides to hang the corner shelf.
6. Scrape all traces of glue, set and fill all nail holes, and proceed to sand the corner shelf to a smooth surface.
7. Select and apply the colored stain or paint of your choice. When dry, apply several coats of lacquer, rubbing between each coat with fine steel wool or pumice and oil. To protect the finish apply a coat of paste wax and buff.

PICTURE FRAME

Materials Required

Part	Number	Size	Material
side	2	¼" x 2" x 20¾"	walnut or the wood of your choice
end	2	¾" x 2" x 16"	
corrugated fasteners	4	½"	
glue			

Picture Frame Plans

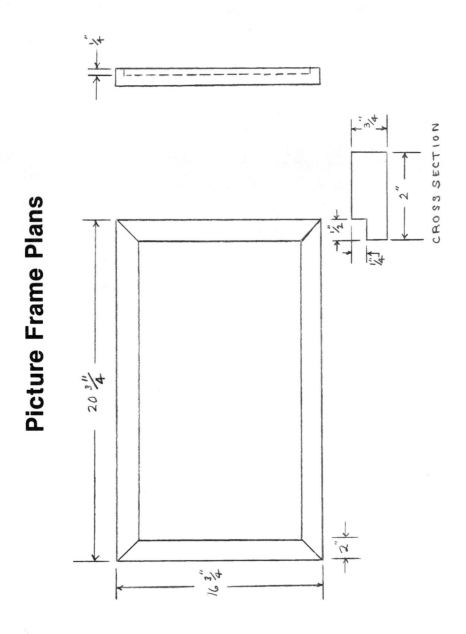

CROSS SECTION

PICTURE FRAME

Procedure

1. Lay out and cut the four pieces to the size indicated.
2. Lay out and cut a ¼ x ½–inch rabbet cut on the inside edge of each piece.
3. Set the miter box to a 45–degree angle, then cut the miter joints to connect the four pieces.
4. Assemble the frame with glue and ½–inch corrugated fasteners fastened to the back side of each miter joint. If corrugated fasteners are not to be used for fastening the miter joint, 1–inch finishing brads may be installed through the corner.
5. Scrape the glue clean, set and fill all nail holes, then sand the frame to a smooth surface.
6. Select and apply the stain or paint of your choice. When dry, apply several coats of finishing oil, rubbing between each coat with fine steel wool or pumice and oil. Protect the finish by applying a coat of paste wax and buffing.

LAMINATED PEN SETS

54

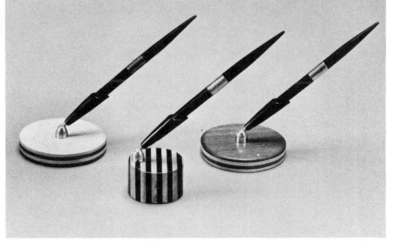

Materials Required

Part	Number	Size	Material
Vertical Design			
strips	6	1¼" x ¼" x 2¼"	maple
strips	6	1¼" x ¼" x 2¼"	walnut
fountain pen	1		
socket swivel	1		
Horizontal Design			
strips	2	³⁄₁₆" x 4"	maple
strips	2	³⁄₁₆" x 4"	walnut
fountain pen	1		
socket swivel	1		

Note: Pens and swivels are available at craft supply stores.

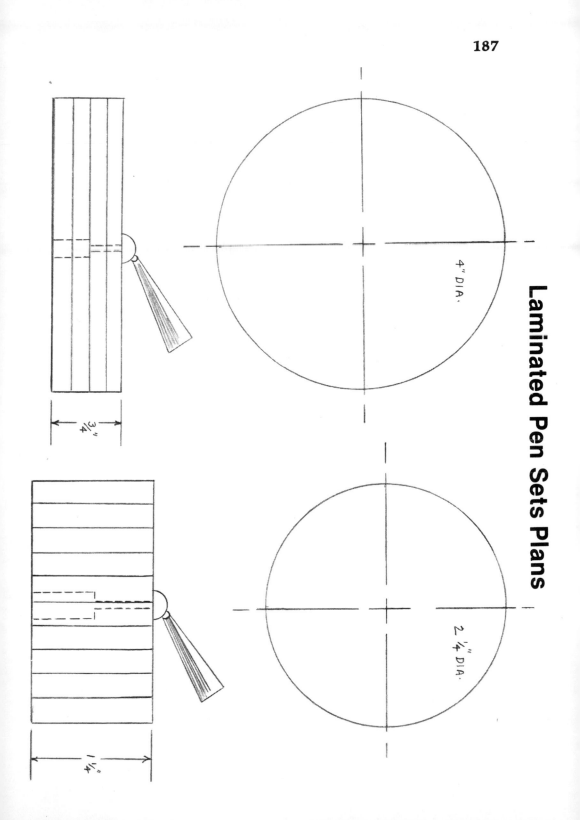

Laminated Pen Sets Plans

4" DIA.

3/4"

2 1/4" DIA.

1 1/4"

LAMINATED PEN SETS

Procedure

1. Select the design of your choice, then continue to cut the correct number of maple and walnut pieces.
2. Glue up and clamp the correct number of hardwood pieces for the design of your choice. When dry, scrape and plane the laminated surface.
3. Lay out and cut the design of your choice.
4. Locate the center, then drill a $\frac{1}{8}$–inch completely through. Counterbore directly over the $\frac{1}{8}$–inch hole with a $\frac{3}{8}$–inch drill to a depth of $\frac{5}{8}$ inches.
5. Sand the laminated disk to a smooth surface, then apply several coats of clear finishing oil, rubbing between coats with fine steel wool or pumice and oil. Protect the finish by applying a coat of paste wax and buffing.
6. Attach the socket swivel with a threaded bolt through the counterbored pilot hole.

BOOK BIN WITH DRAWER

Materials Required

Part	Number	Size	Material
back	1	½ " x 12" x 20"	pine or the wood of your coice
side	2	½ " x 8½ " x 11¼ "	
shelf	2	½ " x 8" x 19½ "	
front piece	2	½ " x 1" x 3"	

Drawer parts:

front and back	2	⅜ " x 2³⁄₁₆ " x 18⅛ "	
side	2	⅜ " x 2³⁄₁₆ " x 7½ "	
false front	1	½ " x 2⁹⁄₁₆ " x 18⅞ "	
bottom	1	⅜ " x 7½ " x 18⅞ "	
nails		#4 finishing	
brads		1" finighing	
glue			
knobs	2	¾ " dia.	birch or the wood of your choice

Book Bin With Drawer Plans

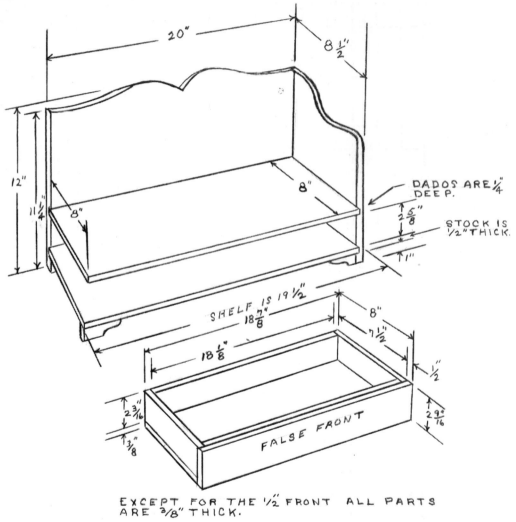

20"

8 1/2"

12"

11 1/4"

8"

8"

8"

DADOS ARE 1/4"
DEEP.

2 5/8"

STOCK IS
1/2" THICK.

1"

SHELF IS 19 1/2"

18 7/8"

18 1/8"

8"

7 1/2"

1/2"

2 3/16"

2 9/16"

1 3/8"

FALSE FRONT

EXCEPT FOR THE 1/2" FRONT ALL PARTS
ARE 3/8" THICK.